WHO PUT THE "P" IN PNEUMONIA?

a kids' book for grown-ups

Mr. Whimsy

WHO PUT THE "P" IN PNEUMONIA

a kids' book for grown-ups

Published in the United States of America
© 2018 marc frederic
All rights reserved

No part of this publication may be reproduced or stored in a retrieval system or transmitted in any form or by any means, electronic, mechanical, photocopying, recording or otherwise, without written permission of the publisher or Marc Frederic, except by reviewer who may quote brief passages in a review.

Permission requests should be emailed to:
mr.whimsy@worldofwhimsy.com

ISBN 13:978-1727377293
10:172737729X

FIRST U.S. EDITION
December 2019

WHO PUT THE P IN *PNEUMONIA*?

Who put the P in *pneumonia*?
And who stuck the K in *knife*?
These are some typical mysteries
I now seem to notice in life.
"Who cares?" you may question sincerely,
"There are loftier matters, no doubt."
I agree some may be more important.
But I've already figured *those* out!

Mr. Whimsy

CHANGING A HABIT

It takes two to four weeks to change a habit.

>It's a nice thing to know
>that it can be done;
>but sounds somewhat slow,
>if one is a nun.

Who Put the "P" in Pneumonia?

CONTRAST

Your hair is clipped and curly, while hers is long and straight.
She's tall and blond and lanky. You're short and overweight.
She's graceful and a beauty. You're kind of pretty too.
She's calm and easy-going. You're nervous through and through
Her nose is Roman classic, while yours is short and stout.
My love for you is equal. It's hard to figure out.
Suppose it stands to reason. I love you both, by golly;
'cause you're my tiny poodle and she's my great big collie.

First printed in
Rainbows, Butterflies and Other Assorted Edibles

Mr. Whimsy

COLORED AIR

Wouldn't it be special,
a vision feast so rare,
I thought in May one windy day,
if we had colored air?
Lemon-yellow breezes,
orange and chartreuse sneezes;
and rainbows when the wind
whirls through your hair.
How wild this world would be with colored air!
Tangerine tornadoes,
lilac Winds of Trade,
gusts and blows like fashion shows;
and gales of pink and jade.
Butterflies and swallows' tails
would leave hue swoops and flutter trails.
And think of all the brilliance in the shade.
Oh, yes, with colored air we'd have it made.

It might have been just like that
till one day someone said,
Oh, wouldn't it be wondrous,
if air were clear instead?
No more tinted raindrops,
no more madras roof tops;
and no more patterns swirling 'round your head.
How marvelous, if air were clear instead!
Colors would be stable,
gardens wouldn't run.
A dress of white would remain bright;
and painting would be fun.

Who Put the "P" in Pneumonia?

All could see for miles around;
separate colors would abound.
Blue would be just blue, and red be red.
How marvelous, if air were clear instead!

Yes, that's how I explain it,
all about the air—
its clarity, its colors and its "suches".
So now that you're aware
and if, of course, you dare,
try thinking 'bout the many tastes of touches.

Mr. Whimsy

BIG PARTS

The giraffe has, by far, the tallest of necks.
The elephant sports a huge nose.
The anteater's tongue is a long, sticky one.
And the sloth has a great set of toes.
The rabbit grows very large ears for its size;
the kangaroo, gigantic tail.
The owl's face is filled with enormous night eyes.
And how 'bout the smile of a whale!
These creatures are special. They're sort of the same—
they all have some very BIG parts.
But you I like best, for you are my friend
and YOU have the biggest of hearts.

INFINITY

Point your finger at a star—
at the end of your arm is your hand.
At the end of your hand is your finger.
That's easy to understand.
At the end of your finger is lots of space
all the way to the star.
From point to point we've measured
be it close or very far.
Now imagine what is past the star,
farther than you can see.
And farther than that—
and farther than that—
as far as far can be.
Is there an end? Is there a wall?
"Of course!" I've heard it cried.
To which I've answered, "Very well,
what's on the other side?"
We haven't yet discovered
an end that cannot be,
but when it's sought, that is the thought
we call *infinity*.

Mr. Whimsy

HOME HUNTING

I've climbed to our kitchen cabinets,
got down every glass and each cup.
I've seventeen pets to find homes for.
Not one is a kitten or pup.
The carnival's where I won them.
You've guessed it. They're all gold fishes.
Oh, quickly! I've got to find bowls;
the rims are too low on our dishes.
Now where are our jars and vases?
I'm sorry, I really must rush.
My dad just suggested the toilet
and said he'd be happy to flush!

Who Put the "P" in Pneumonia?

I THINK IN YOU I'VE FOUND ONE

I think in you I've found one.
Yes, you truly are a friend.
Your loyalty's amazing
and 'round obstacles you bend.
You never push or crowd me
yet, you heed my every move.
You love the sun as I do.
On that we can't improve.
Today when we were running
and I cast you in the sea,
then laughing, drew you out again
to come and play with me,
you shook your head, but followed;
then fell hard upon the sand
and lie there heaving breathlessly,
as I gave you my hand.
There was no hesitation
when my hand you then did take.
I thought about your color—
no difference did it make.
You're silent, dark, a mystery.
We're two halves that make a whole;
and as we stand together
there's a meeting of our soles.
I wish that you could tell me,
for I'd really love to know,
just where it is at night time
that you, my shadow, go.

First printed in
Life Inside an Apostrophe

Mr. Whimsy

ANIMAL GOLF COURSE
RULES AND REGS:

We ask your attire be proper please—
your shirts should have sleeves; your pants reach your knees.
And, if you've no knees from which you can measure,
we ask that you cover your parts that give pleasure.
No talons, spiked toenails or claws that offend.
They tear up our greens which we then have to mend.
Your hooves may make dents or, if heavy, depressions.
No gophers or moles due to tunnel transgressions.
On fairways fill divots. Fix ball marks on greens.
Refrain from loud roaring, blare-bleating and screams.
Please DO use the rest rooms. Please DON'T eat the flowers.
Gorillas, when putting, curtail your great power.
And, cattle, when driving, don't move as a herd;
but "snaking in" putts here is far from absurd.
You're welcome to scout the next hole from the trees
or use as your caddies, giraffes, if you please.
One stroke under par on a hole we call "hummers";
two under, "wonders" and one over, "bummers".
Our restaurant is stocked with the finest of stores
quite easily reached in low troughs on the floors.
This course was created to play and to roam.
Please treat it more kindly than you would your home.

HOW I LOVE PLAYING GOLF!

How I love to play golf! And I truly must say
the more slowly I swing, the much better I play.
It's a concept that's strange for, as everyone knows,
the harder you hit it, the farther it goes.
Yes, that *is* what you'd think. But that's not really right.
No, it's rhythm and tempo, not muscle and might.
It's a smooth, steady weight shift—a coil and return
that can give one a golf swing for which others yearn.
Such a fine way of playing! It makes me feel great,
for an effortless swing and the ball's flying straight.
If I'd just make each shot with these forethoughts in mind,
all my rounds would be splendid…low-scoring…refined.
You would think I'd remember and have no regret.
But for some dog-gone reason, I tend to forget!

Mr. Whimsy

EXERCISING

"Why so happy?" I was asked,
while attempting to stay thin.
I responded candidly,
"That's a grimace, not a grin."

THE HAND

Throughout our lives we learn to look at faces.
Though some may be deceptive, most are grand.
The more I see and more I travel places
a more important thing becomes "the hand".
There's the hand that rocks the cradle. Never knock it.
And the hand dealt from the bottom of the deck;
and the hand that picks the wallet from a pocket;
and the hand that makes a fist or writes a check.
There's the "helping hand" a fella asks you give him
and the hand who works the brand out on the ranch;
and the handyman who tinkers for a livin'
and the hand of God that trips the avalanche.
Yes, the daughter's hand for which you ask her father
and the healing hand that leaves you ailment free;
plus the hand you give to show appreciation
and the sleight of hand which tests credulity.
There's the "first" and "second hand," like how you hear it
and the "hand-me-downs" as found in suit and frock;
'course the "heavy" hand, which cannot lift a spirit,
and the two relentless hands that sweep the clock.
But one hand tops them all the way I see it;
the one that means as much as any can.
The one you clasp in even more than friendship—
the trusted handshake of an honest man.

Mr. Whimsy

THE AMAZON AND THE MANATEE

It's true most manatees swim "slow".
They munch and wander as they go.
But one about the Amazon
said, "What a river! It's right on!
To swim up its great length, you see,
would thrill a manatee like me.
I'm not your average manatee.
I swim as swiftly as can be."
He spoke those words, then glanced around
and seemed to slim his bulk right down.
An eerie sight he came to be—
a sleek and streamlined manatee.
From river's mouth he made his move
and soon was in a steady groove.
He swam right by his bros and sisters
with speed so fast it gave them blisters!
He nipped the hippos' napping short —
not one did yawn, but all did snort.
He shocked the crocs, but felt their smiles
while swimming fifteen-second-miles.
They saw not him, for goodness sake,
but noted well his three-mile wake.
He swam below, but not too deep.
He slowed not once to eat nor sleep.
At last…a sight which made him quiver—
he'd reached the start of this great river!
The Amazon was quite impressed,
"You've swum my length without a rest!
I'm thankful that it's thrills you seek.
Because of you I now can speak.
"You swam so fast," the river said,
"you put my mouth back in my head!
From now until eternity
I'll sing your praise, my manatee."

Who Put the "P" in Pneumonia?

This tale, of course, is fantasy; but nearly all it states could be.
There is one fact that you should know is mentioned here, but isn't so—
though rivers sing and crocs do smile, the hippos live along the Nile.
Please know the Amazon is real and, as a river, has appeal.
No need to get hysterical. It's sort of South Americal.
Through several countries it does spill and ends in one we call Brazil.
The Nile is very far away—a continent or two, I'd say.
Through Africa the Nile does run.
    Check out a map. You'll find it's fun.

Mr. Whimsy

A BEVY OF HOT-AIR BALLOONS

"BALLOONS!
 BALLOONS!"
arose the cry.
Against the blue and golden sky,
across the meadow,
over the hill
appeared the colorful "hot-air" thrill.
HUGE they were—gigantic blooms
from out of the earth;
magnificent moons
which slowly glided above us all
as if en route to a costume ball.
A mystic image,
some magic dreamed
from both the future and past
it seemed.
Like statues we stood
in wonder and awe,
amazed in the silence by what we saw.
We were happy as larks.
We felt crazy as loons.
We will never forget those hot-air balloons,
for, you see, as they drifted
to unknown parts
they captured a bit of our souls and hearts.
Today I remember that "long ago",
as I gaze at the people
far below.
I hang in my basket high in the sky
and know
what they feel
as I hear them cry,
"BALLOONS!
 BALLOONS!"

Who Put the "P" in Pneumonia?

A.B.SEAGULL

A.B., my C-gull,
once asked if it's legal
to change his initials to E.
"To be known as E-gull
would make me feel regal,"
he said. So, I told him, "We'll see."
"Sea!" said my C-gull,
 a sharp paralegal,
"is just where I *don't* want to *be*!"
"B?" I asked Seagull.
 "We're now talking 'beagle'."
 It's all quite confusing to me.

Mr. Whimsy

IF I COULD HAVE THREE WISHES

I'd like to look like Cary Grant but still be me inside.
I'd like to have a billion bucks though I've not really tried.
But just in case that's not enough, like most smart folks would do,
I'd make sure with my final wish all future ones come true.

I LOVE IT UNLIMITED

Why wish for a trickle of water
when God grants waterfalls?
And why visit only the "dime store"
when man's made shopping malls?
Why ask for vanilla ice cream
when flavors are grand/galore?
There's not a thing wrong with vanilla,
but, gee, there are so many more!
Why settle for ten great minutes
when I can have hours and days?
Why strive to earn B's as an average
when I can conceive of straight A's?
Why limit my friends to close ones
when others have so much to give?
Why think only "here" is the best place?
There are wonders wherever I live.
Is the rose more fair than the daisy?
Does the daffodil take first prize?
Who cares? The questions are crazy.
There are Gardens for feasting our eyes.
Does the Rainbow censor its colors?
Does Gravity choose what falls?
Do you think Love cares who shares it?
Infinity has no walls!
I can have as much or as little
of whatever I dare, my friend.
When I put myself in the middle
I am never aware of an end.
It's all right here to enjoy.
with abundance the world is rife.
I'm a fine, deserving being
and I'm treating myself to Life!

Mr. Whimsy

POUNDAGE ON THE PATIO

There's poundage on the patio. I'll sweep it all away.
It's also scattered in our yard. I'll rake it up today.
I try my best to be aware, to round it up without a care.
It truly isn't very rare to find some on the couch or chair.
The ounces left within the sink I rinse away with smiling wink.
It's on the bath mat. I declare! A pound or two upon the stair.
A few more ounces here and there. It virtually is everywhere.
I am amazed she's still in tact. I state it as a simple fact:
       My wife is losing weight, my friend.
        And I'm not one who minds it.
         I stash all I can apprehend.
       And hope she never finds it.

Who Put the "P" in Pneumonia?

MY STAND-OFFISH FRIEND

Black Sammy, our cat, though he's cuddly tame,
can, at times, be extremely aloof.
He shuts his green eyes, as I'm calling his name—
an insulting example of proof.
He'll, at times, turn his back, being nonchalant cool,
and casually walk straight away.
Thus, though *he's* well-adored, he makes *me* feel ignored,
which surely does not make my day!
But whenever he's hungry or just feels inclined,
he snuggles and purrs to no end.
This makes me feel good, just as he knew it would.
So I treat him like he's my best friend.

Mr. Whimsy

PEACES

So many pieces has the puzzle—
a warm, blue sea…a loving nuzzle…
companionship…a job well done…
the gift of praise…a race well run…
a snowfall's calm…a verse well-turned…
a spiritual oneness learned.
Mosaic wonders never cease.
Would you please add a little peace?

HAPPINESS HECTOR
(the Bad Dream Collector)

Once upon a time, in the shimmering land of Shand-o-Meer, a pixie married an elf. They had 13 children—six pixies, six elves, and a pelf. They named the pelf Hector.

The family was a happy one. Hector was, by far, the happiest of all. He was filled with happiness from the tips of his toes to the top of his head. He giggled happiness. He winked happiness. All his thoughts were happy ones.

His brother and sister pixies eventually danced off to play in colorful flower gardens. His sibling elves travelled to Santa's workshop to create wonderful toys.

Hector wasn't sure where to go. He only knew he was full of happiness and wanted to share it. But how?

Hector thought long and hard. He imagined many ways to make this world a happier place.

At last the answer came to him—rid the world of bad dreams. To do so, he would use his inherited magical powers.

From imagination threads, he weaves a small pouch to be placed under the pillow of every girl and boy. With it he leaves a wish for the children to let any unwanted dreams fly into the pouch when Mommy or Daddy tucks them into bed or kisses them goodnight.

As the children drift off to sleep, Hector collects those discarded visions. He drops them into his silent dream-disposal. There they turn and tumble, churn and crumble, until they are minced into pieces so small they disappear. To these nothings he adds fairy dust that creates the lovely, beautiful, warm and happy dreams he leaves under pillows for everyone to enjoy.

And to this very evening, all who believe in Happiness Hector the Bad Dream Collector sleep safely, snuggled in comfortable, happy feelings. All night long.

Mr. Whimsy

"ASTONISHING"

"Astonishing,"
"endorphins,"
"fond" and "tyke"
are simply words
I've overheard
and that I sort of like.
Of course, so many others
I love to hear & say,
but those that I've just mentioned
caressed my ears today.

Who Put the "P" in Pneumonia?

BLUE

Of the world's many blues I have been asked to choose
just exactly which one I like best.
It's a chore I adore. What a thrill to explore!
It has been a most marvelous quest.
I have known blue as neon 'neath snow that I ski on.
I have found it in dazzling fish.
There's the blue of a flame. And in flowers, I claim,
there is most any shade one may wish.
'Course the butterfly's wing (a magnificent thing)
and the shimmer of humming bird's throat
are but two fine examples of lovely blue samples
most certainly worthy of note.
I have rowed to and fro in Blue Grotto below
the world famous Isle of Capri.
I have seen the stars rise in a maiden's blue eyes
who has fallen in deep love with me.
I have shed a sad tear over "blues" that I hear
in the wail of a brass saxophone;
and have viewed the blue dance in the gems of romance
as the fire of many a stone.
I have searched from up high in the Idaho sky
to the shallows of tropical seas
where I've found powder blue, royal, turquoise too—
any number of tones, which do please.
But the greatest of blues, of all rich and soft hues;
yes, the finest! To which I will drink.
Is the one that I've found after looking around
in the mouth of a small blue-tongued skink.

Mr. Whimsy

ANIMAL COLLECTIVE NAMES

Animals fascinate us.
Their forms and habits breed fame.
When grouped quite closely, some species
are given an intriguing name.
Several are very dramatic.
Many are practical, too.
Some names are cute, others a hoot;
here is a list of a few:
A group of goldfishes is called *a glint*;
a group of giraffes is a *tower*.
It's fun and amazing how much can be meant
by subtly using word power.
A *pack* of wolves we know for sure,
but a *dazzle* of zebras. Oh, my!
A *purse* of sand dollars and *cling* of koalas
so aptly exemplify.
A *constellation* of star fish.
A group of trout is a *hover*.
A *lounge* of lizards. A *wake* of buzzards.
How many there are to discover!
A *bloat* of hippopotami and
a *bask* of crocodiles sound good.
But a *murder* of crows may disturb you,
as a *crash* of rhinoceros would.
On the other hand, there are more quite grand:
a *prickle* of porcupines,
a *scurry* of squirrels, a *gaze* of raccoons
and, of course, a *pride* of lions.
They make cute pets to cuddle
and often they're even adored,
but hamsters as well as gerbils,
when collectives are labeled a *horde*.

Who Put the "P" in Pneumonia?

A guinea pig group is a *muddle;*
an armadillos' a *role;*
an otter*s'* a *romp;* Pekinese are a *pomp*
and a *labor's* the group name for moles.
You may think it's odd that a whale group's a *pod*
or a group of tigers, a *streak.*
There are so many more you may wish to explore.
On the internet do take a peek.
Under *Animal Groups* you will find *broods* and *troops,*
a colony, covey and *nest,*
a company, gaggle, a huddle or puddle),
It's hard to decide which is best.
In addition to *clutches, warrens* in hutches,
a *herd,* a *band* and a *bed,*
there are swarms and *schools, tribes, knots* and *clews.*
So many to fill your head.
A *fleet,* a *parade.* This wild cavalcade
can eventually lead to confusion.
A *plague,* a *cloud.* And, for crying out loud,
for cockroaches they list *intrusion*!
But Lord only knows that I cannot close
this verse without quoting some dandies.
For to me, you see, these names can be
as sweet as assortments of candies.
There are *leaps* of leopards, *charms* of finches,
scolds of jays and such;
ostentations of peacocks, *bamboos* of pandas.
Each has a colorful touch.
The cormorants' *gulp.* A *stand* of flamingos.
Even the mallards' *brace.*
Some are exotic, most are exquisite.
Few are just commonplace.
Bouquets of pheasants. A *bevy* of swans.
A *parliament* of owls.
A *quiver* of cobras. A *shiver* of sharks.
And many group names for fowls.
A *bloom* of jellyfish. *Scourge* of mosquitoes.
Hyenas' *cackle* or *clan.*

Mr. Whimsy

>A *mischief* of mice. A butterfly *flutter*.
>And camels' *caravan*.
>A *run* of salmon. *Pandemonium* of parrots.
>Also, an *army* of ants.
>An amazing array! What more can I say?
>It fascinates, even enchants.
>A *cluster* of spiders. A *cast* of crabs.
>A *fever* of rays that sting.
>What I'd planned to do was list just a few,
>but that's almost everything.

Who Put the "P" in Pneumonia?

INDISCERNIBLE

The zebras' stripes enhance their skin
in sun and rainy weather.
Can't tell justwheretheyendbegin
when they stand close together!

Mr. Whimsy

I'M SO SORE

I thought that with *yoga*
my body I'd etch.
It turned out to be a
bit m-u-c-h o-f a
s—t—-r——e———-t————-c————-h ! ! !

Who Put the "P" in Pneumonia?

I'M DROGGY

I've taken my pills and I'm droggy.
They make   me weel that fay.
I quite dunno what I'm taying,
and con't dare anyway.
I took'em a bittle lit early.
The doc says take'em at niiight.
Eye no I should due what he sezzzz but
they make my dreams a sight,
for WORDS hang in the windows
and thoughts creep under the rug
and sounds are long. They warble wrong.
CONFUSION tastes like bugs.
The meter, which constantly changes,
will have nothing to do with the rhyme.
And granite notes of music floats
through cracks we've made in time.
I sing a roast beef sandwich. Geraniums I sigh.
A royal pink potato now rides a butterfly.
The walls are kinda smushy.
I'm sleeping in a song.
Its bars are made of rubber; it wears a red sarong.
There's so much more to tell you,
but who cares what I say?
I'm really very droggy.
Not much makes sense today.

Inspired by its first line, which was said to me
on the phone by my mother-in-law.

Mr. Whimsy

THE PENGUIN DIFFERS FROM THE PUFFIN

The penguin dresses formally.
That's obvious for all to see.
And, yet, he feels quite put-upon
to fly with his tuxedo on.
He, therefore, walks when he must go
to fancy parties in the snow,
but dreams of soaring here and there,
of "going casual" everywhere.
His outfit he may wish to doff,
but he can't get the darn thing off!

The puffin is a different breed
from penguin. That we must concede.
In dinner jacket he may dress,
yet flies with no apparent stress.
Propelling through the air with ease,
he dives to swim beneath the seas.
In fact, it is his fervent wish
to fill his bill with rows of fish,
which he then wings while hardly huffin'
home for baby puffin stuffin'.

Who Put the "P" in Pneumonia?

RAINBOW BEING
(The Crayon Eater)

An odd Crayon Eater lives under my bed.
She colors my dreams every night.
And, though I've not seen her, I have heard it said
she's truly a very strange sight.
She's colorful, yes; and surely well-fed.
She shimmers in many a hue;
and three of her eyes are orange, green and red;
the others, pink, yellow and blue.
She changes quite often. It must be inherent.
In day time she's light as can be.
In fact, it's apparent that she is transparent—
right through her my friends and I see.
But then, late at night she becomes quite a sight.
Her hair's multicolored spaghetti
while out of her ears float grenadine tears
and her mouth chuckles puffs of confetti.
She bumbles and mumbles and tumbles around.
Of this, I am rather aware.
She makes gentle noises and comforting sounds.
In fact, I am glad she is there.
She's told me about her; just how she appears,
how I should not see her at night.
If I peer directly, she says that she fears
I might have a horrible fright.
So I must confess. I don't peek in the dark.
She's nice but she's given me warning
and cleans up her mess without a remark
before I awake every morning.

Mr. Whimsy

DANCES

The macarena's danced by those
who like to shake their butts.
The hula's danced, I do suppose,
by macadamia nuts.
Does this mean the insania
is trotted to by foxes
and that the jumpamania's
performed by jacks in boxes?

DRAGON IN THE ARCTIC

A wizard instructed, then gave me my pick
of whom I would work with to pull off his trick.
I've chosen a Dragon. Its breath's mighty nice—
it keeps me so toasty amidst all this ice.
The Dragon and I have a mission quite bold—
to please a great giant who is HUGE I am told.
My friend's a big help when quenching Giant's thirst.
And that is precisely why I chose him first.
We're here in the Arctic—"retrievers" I think,
to bring home a glacier to cool the giant's drink!
He drinks from a lake instead of a flagon.
My friend understands this and, though I'm not braggin',
we haven't a sled, nor even a wagon
and, yet, we're on schedule. We're surely not laggin'.
We're fine glacier movers who never need naggin'
'cause I'm good at pushin' and he's great at draggin'.

Mr. Whimsy

ELEVATOR ATTITUDE

The doors slide open. In I step.
The riders seem to have no pep.
A solemn hush engulfs the crowd.
These folks don't dare to think out loud.
Each single person has his space
and sports a blank look on his face.
All turned to front, they stare up high
to watch the numbered lights go by.
I promise one day, soon or later
I'll step inside that elevator
and just to be some sort of clown
I'll look at them and not turn 'round.
I'll talk or sing or tell short jokes
or possibly I'll question folks.
But when they reach their destined floors,
and then depart through the sliding doors,
I'll turn and stand as if I'm dead—
so silent, staring straight ahead.
Just why do we all act this way?
Psychologists might simply say
it's nature's mode of lending grace
to people in too little space.
On other folks they won't intrude
and, thus, their actions are subdued.
They'll not be viewed as being rude,
do nothing that's construed as crude.
Not even sneezes do elude
this "elevator attitude."

Who Put the "P" in Pneumonia?

EASTER EGGS

Just why is it
(I sure hope YOU know)
the Easter Bunny leaves eggs?
He *could* leave bananas,
or lamb chops or jewels
or packets of scorpion legs.
And why in the world does he hide them
after painting them, oh, so bright?
And why in the world should a bunny
be hopping around through the night?
Well,
bananas can get a bit mushy.
And lamb chops one can not paint.
Jewels cost a lot. And like it or not,
scorpion-lovers we ain't.
So beautiful eggs are hidden.
And the reason for this, it is said,
is if you should see all these treasures at once,
your eyes would pop out of your head.
But why are they left by a rabbit?
I've narrowed the answer to one—
if they were delivered by tortoise,
it would take farrrrrr tooooooo lo-o-o-o-o-ng
 to get done.

Mr. Whimsy

THE EVIL WEEVIL AND THE LADYBUG

"I'm an Evil Weevil from Bugville
but you oughta see me strut my stuff.
I'm an Evil Weevil from Bug Town
and you better believe I'm tough!
For lunch I eat a cottonwood tree
then spit Q-tips till half past three.
I'm an Evil Weevil from Bugville
but you oughta see me strut my stuff."

"I'm Ladybug Little from the country,
and Bugville's quite a town!
I'm a sweet and naïve farm bug;
don't know my way around.
But, Sir, if you'd be kind enough
to show me how to strut my stuff,
I'd be ever in your debt, Sir,
for I'm a little ladybug."

Now together they stroll to the Match Box
where the other bugs are dancin' up a storm.
The Big Bee Band is blarin'
more like *hot* than warm!
The long-legged Spider strums his web
while the Praying Mantis croons
and it all comes together, it might be said,
in a swarm of Bugville tunes.
The Weevil looks around, gives a little shrug
and proceeds to cut a rug with the Ladybug.
Then they drink sarsaparilla with a glug, glug, glug
till the Lady asks to dance again.

Who Put the "P" in Pneumonia?

Oh, they whirl and they twirl
and they twirl and they swirl
and they dance till the break of dawn.
Long after that Weevil is plumb worn out
the Ladybug keeps right on!

Ladybug, Ladybug! What a dame!
You put that Weevil all to shame
and sent him packin', lookin' lame,
from the Bug Town Strutters Hall.

The place goes wild when the Weevil splits
'cause they don't like him. Not one bit.
And they crowd around Miss Ladybug
just a-tryin' to give her a kiss and hug.

"Well, the Weevil's gone and that is keen,
but things aren't always as they seem.
Can those kisses! Hold that hug!
'Cause I'm no lady, I'm a Jitter Bug!"

Mr. Whimsy

EYE GLASSES

You, glasses, are my buddy—
you're into being snug.
I do believe you love me.
You sure know how to hug—
you reach your arms out to me,
then slide them 'round my face
and all day long you hold me
in such a sweet embrace.
I love you, too, eye glasses.
You really help me see.
If not for you, my classes
would be a blur to me.

EYES ARE FANTASTIC

Eyes are fantastic.
Nays are not bad.
Both can be happy,
both can be sad;
My friend, the answer isn't
in the things, themselves, that be;
it's simply in our vision
and the beauty that we see.

Mr. Whimsy

IF YOU'LL

If you'll
plant a kiss,
I'll cultivate
the garden.

First printed in
Strawberry Glue

Who Put the "P" in Pneumonia?

GARDENING

Lyin' in the warm sun
sippin' on a brew,
gettin' high
on perfumed skies,
and makin' eyes at you.
Breezes trim the hedges,
butterflies do garden.
I can see
the busy bee
my indolence does pardon.
Song birds sing my love song,
hummingbird's my fan.
In palm trees' shade
I've got it made.
Please pass another can.

Mr. Whimsy

The
Immediate Result
of
Infinite Patience
is

PEACE

May it be yours

(from *A Course in Miracles*)

AUTOGRAPH PARTY

What a marvelous autograph party!
It all seemed to work out just right.
The crowds weren't the least bit tardy;
the children, all bright and polite.
The store had done advertising
by phone and, of course, internet.
Their signage both inside and outside
was surely as good as you get.
The owner did film my performance,
which truly was one of a kind,
for no one was in attendance.
The glamour was all in my mind.
It was something just plain unexpected.
The owner was red in the face
but, more or less poised, not dejected.
In fact, she exhibited grace.
She suggested I read for the camera
and caught all my words without fans,
then offered to send me a copy
to try to make up for failed plans.
Though not even one book did sell,
'twas the merest of minor disasters.
My time getting home worked out well
to watch Tiger Woods in *The Masters'*!

Mr. Whimsy

AVENUE OF THE REDWOODS
(on the Oregon coast)

At first I feel quite lost and small
amidst these redwood giants so tall.
The sky seems, oh, so far away,
as if the night might steal the day.
But as my eyes and soul adjust,
such monumental size I trust.
I am protected and elite—
alone, yet mothered at their feet.
The warmth and colors have combined
to soothe my soul, caress my mind.
Enveloped now in ferns of green,
I find the forest so serene.
My eyes, indeed, now fill my heart
with Nature's splendid works of art.
Just taste the colors! Look around!
For here God's palette does abound—
magenta, plum, the black of bear;
a sunray softly streaks the air,
as one collides, no doubt it must,
with bark of tree; explodes in rust-
vermillion-gold. Such stunning hues,
contrasting with the pinks and blues.
The brook just chuckles on and long
while birds enchant the woods with song.
This ancient forest, I'm aware,
is my great privilege to share.
Its gentle giants, so filled with grace
create a spirit-merging place.

Who Put the "P" in Pneumonia?

It cradles me within its arms.
It overwhelms me with its charms.
My soul will never say "adieu"
to this, the *Redwood Avenue.*

Written while gazing at a painting by Violet Parkhurst 2003

Mr. Whimsy

THE GIFT

I'd come home from college for Christmas that year.
Our household was filled with much love and good cheer.
One evening I sat with my dad watching news—
we laughed, we talked and tippled some booze.
It was then that he offered, with heart in his eye,
a thing I'll embrace till the day that I die —
he told how he treasured his tiny T-bird
and I'd have one like it, if I gave the word.
I wanted to take it, as sure as I'm living;
I thought of the car and Dad's pleasure in giving.
But take it I couldn't. I felt wrong inside.
I just hadn't earned it, and had too much pride.
I then wasn't working and Dad paid for school.
The thought of this gift made me feel like a fool.
I told of the students making straight A's.
Some broke but, through scholarships they earned their ways.
I told him of rich ones who almost flunked out
and the sleek new corvettes that they sported about.
I admitted I work just as hard as I please;
my grades consist only of C's and some B's;
in scholastic endeavors I'm surely no star;
and my hang outs are women's apartments and bars.
My dad said he realized just where I stood.
I knew he did care and his mind was quite good.
I was torn by the trauma of which way to turn.
My thoughts became twisted; my guts seemed to churn.
Then all became brilliance, bright rays through the cloud,
as my father said gently, "Don't always be proud.
Take the car, and grow into the man who you feel
would deserve to be sitting behind such a wheel.
At the time you have done so, you'll know it is right."
I was stunned and amazed by the man's great insight

.

Who Put the "P" in Pneumonia?

I walked to and hugged him, my eyes filled with tears.
We stood and, in silence, held each other dear.
To this day I marvel at what Dad had done —
such a beautiful gift from a man to his son.

Mr. Whimsy

THE HERMIT

On the side of the hill
at the end of the shade of the tree
sat a sad little man
with his arm 'twixt his chin and his knee.
There were rakes strewn all around,
several shovels on the ground,
and a purple velvet bag as big as me.
I asked, "Sir, why so glum?"
He sighed, "From a cave I come.
I've lived there sixteen years and seven days.
I'm a hermit, son, by trade
and I've always had it made
until ambition sort of changed my ways.
Now I'm not much of a digger
but I saw my cave as bigger
so I started clawin' chunks right off the walls.
Pretty soon it looked right nifty
and, bein' kinda thrifty,
I *stopped*   at thirty rooms and two great halls.
Now you ask why I'm so glum.
Well, it may seem sorta dumb
but that mountain's made of yellow shiny stuff.
Sure, I've now got lots of space
in my brand new livin' place
but the sparklin' makes the sleepin' mighty tough.
I've almost blown my fuse
figurin' just what I could use
to dull that glitter down so's I can sleep.
It's got to be real black
and fit in this here sack;
and, since I got no dough, it must be cheap.
And then it came to me—
there's plenty and they're free!

Who Put the "P" in Pneumonia?

So I've run right here to where you see me sad.
Each day I've watched 'em grow.
By now I feel I know
just where the best of them are to be had.
I'll claim them for my own.
I'll take them shadows home
and smudge them on the walls with my old rag.
You see, I've got the tools.
But, maybe they're a fool's,
'cause I can't get them durn things in my bag!

Mr. Whimsy

ENJOY

I enjoy
people
the way
most people
enjoy books—
ever curl up
with a good
person?

First printed in
Life Inside An Apostrophe

I COULD SIT ALL EVENING

I could just sit all evening
knowing you'd be close to me.
Your taste and mine together
go so very perfectly.
Your legs are so damn tempting
and your body's fine as well.
I'd love to get much closer,
if you'd come out of your shell.
I don't know what it is
that makes me drool and want to grab.
I guess it's 'cause I'm hungry
and you're a cold cracked crab.

First published in
Rainbows, Butterflies and Other Assorted Edibles

Mr. Whimsy

COLORFUL FRIENDS

I like Juba.
Her skin is so blue.
Milla is pink.
And she's pretty too.
Gantar is handsome.
He's striped and has dots.
Sinta's skin glows
with spectacular spots.
My skin looks best when I
let the sun tan it.
I love how we differ
from planet to planet.

Who Put the "P" in Pneumonia?

COLOR BLIND?

We thought our son was color blind. He mixed up all the hues.
Reds he saw as yellow shades and greens he said were blues.
Brown it seemed to him was orange. And purple he called pink.
This went on till he was three. We weren't sure what to think.
So to the "Doc" we took our son to learn what he did see.
The Doc told us he had a test as simple as can be.
He then brought out a jar of glass and filled it to the brim
with many colored candy pills. The brand was "M&M."
He told our son that he could have a candy colored green.
That piece was grabbed about as fast as anything we'd seen!
The test took several minutes. To us it all seemed weird
for, as he called each color's name, the candy disappeared!
About the color—blindness we never had to fuss.
We simply learned we had a child who was quite devious!

Mr. Whimsy

ADVENTURE

Last night I shared an adventure.
I'll never again be the same.
Our five-year-old son, little Eric,
I took to his first baseball game.
Arriving a half-hour early
and finding our seats as we planned,
I left him to watch batting practice
while I raided the hot dog stand.
I returned armed with goodies and answers
to the questions I thought he'd ask soon.
But rather than ball field and players
his attention was caught by the moon.
I told how six outs made an inning.
I pointed to bases and mound.
My son's eyes grew big as two saucers
as the cracker jack man made his round.
We stood for the national anthem;
then just 'fore the first pitch was fired,
as applause brought the game's beginning,
my son informed me he was tired.
First inning was very eventful.
the Dodgers led three runs to "O."
Besides, during all the excitement
my son kicked my beer with his toe!

No matter, I'll soon get another.
There's much more still left to enjoy.
How often do I get to share this—
an outing alone with our boy?
His next question really did throw me,
"Dad, the vampire bit whose behind?"

Who Put the "P" in Pneumonia?

I suppose in the heat of the action
I had just called the umpire blind.
And even though I then explained it
the image roamed wild in his head;
for the next time I looked he was drawing
a dragon "to hang o'er his bed."
I knew from all of the hot dogs
and cokes and candy that soon,
about when the game became tied up,
he'd ask me to go to "the room".
And so, I sat there and waited…
and sure as it had to be,
the Pirates got their game together
and tied up the score three to three.
'Twas just about this time I felt it.
I was somewhat reluctant to peek,
for into my lap he was crawling.
He panted a kiss on my cheek.
He gave me the grandest of hugs then
and snuggled his head to my chest,
while in a soft voice he informed me,
"Gee, Dad, you're really the best."
We watched as the Pirates took it.
To him it was all so-so.
He clapped as the winning run scored
and asked, "Daddy, now can we go?"
He almost got lost in the shuffle
but made it back from whence we came.
And, though he had done many fun things,
I *think* he enjoyed the *game.*

First printed in
Rainbows, Butterflies and Other Assorted Edibles

Mr. Whimsy

THE BAT IN OUR ROOM

A bat flew into our room last night.
It startled us with its flappy flight.
It hit the wall with a little thud.
We jumped away to save our blood!
Though in a tropical hotel,
we did not summon "Personnel."
I must admit, at first we swore,
then shooed that bat right out the door.
It truly was a happening,
a strange and crazy sort of thing.
What reason? What does this all mean?
A remnant left from Halloween?
And why OUR room? I figure that
it must have been our turn at bat!

First printed in
The Enticing Wonder of Gaylan

Who Put the "P" in Pneumonia?

BLOOD LEVEL

No wonder I've been feeling "slow"—
I've just been told I'm 2 pints low!
And, though I feel it's academic,
the doctor says that I'm anemic.
And then, to add to the confusion,
"I just may need a quick transfusion"—
with hemoglobin over nine,
I temporarily am fine;
but under nine, they'll "pop my bubble"
by stressing that I'm in deep trouble.
So here I wait. It is my quest
to learn the level of my test…

Results come in at 8.9
indicating I'm not fine.
For years I've thought it's really great
to roll up sleeve and then donate.
But now, it seems, I'll have a crack
at getting some of that blood back!

Mr. Whimsy

BREAKFAST

I've just been laid, he happily boasted,
and you, my friend, will soon be toasted.
That's what the chicken egg just said
to the slice of whole wheat bread.
I'd much rather be freshly squeezed
than represent the old deep freeze,
bubbled the orange juice to the glass,
now let's prepare to show some class.
Quit spooning with the fork, you knife.
Such boldness I've seldom seen in my life!
Shape up, or action will be taken,
you'll be splattered by the bacon!
Batter up, please, it's pancake time.
Hello, Hash Brown, you're looking fine.
Good morning, Sugar, how's my sweet?
When you sprinkle this morning, try to be neat.
And, Creamer, please don't spill a drop.
Hurry up now, the snoring has stopped!
Believe it or not, I could have sworn
I heard those words from the kitchen this morn.
But I can't help think, as I rose from bed,
some dreams were still lurking inside my head.

First printed in
Rainbows, Butterflies and Other Assorted Edibles

Who Put the "P" in Pneumonia?

BRAIN SCAN

I'm here to have my brain well-scanned.
I wonder what they'll see.
Most likely shapes and colors grand
as happy as can be.
My wife thinks my recall's declined.
That's why I'm here today.
But when they peer inside my mind,
they'll smile and cheer, "HOORAY!"
They will be inundated
with thoughts and visions rare.
No, nothing overrated,
just lovely things with flair.
"Why, look what he's created!"
they'll point and laugh and shout.
They'll be so fascinated
they won't want to come out!

Mr. Whimsy

COLORING

I'll have some blue, please.
Pass me that tear.
No, the lighter one,
the one with the laugh in it.
That's it. Now the pink,
the little girl's kiss.
I don't need the whole jar;
just blow some over here.
I smell mango-orange,
it's there, under the dandelion.
Please don't move rapidly;
you'll change notes in the melody.
A sprig of dill;
no, no, I mean mint,
and a baby's smile
should lend the right tint.
Ah, yes. Now the frame.
It'll be hard to find.
Is it asking too much
to please borrow your mind?

First printed in
Rainbows, Butterflies and Other Assorted Edibles

Who Put the "P" in Pneumonia?

AFTER THE PARTY

After the party we help straighten up—
put wayward cupcakes back in their cups,
make sure the napkins are taking their naps
and all the pop bottles are wearing their caps,
stick all the candles back in their can,
match up each spic with its very own span,
sail all the streamers far up their streams,
turn down the volume of all the ice screams.
Make sure the presents are not in the past
and the fin is on "finished", for that is the last.

Mr. Whimsy

BLOODY EYEBALL GHOULASH

Bloody eyeball ghoulash. It's such a special treat—
a heavy, hearty, Halloweeny stew.
Taste, but as you sup it, watch closely what you eat;
for there's no doubt it will be watching you.

Who Put the "P" in Pneumonia?

BAD DREAM

*Tiny, rapid footsteps
pounding down the hall—
by our bed our son stands
less than four feet tall.*
What's the matter, Honey?
rubbing at my eyes.
Had a bad dream, Daddy,
he tearfully replies.
Well, everything is all right.
Let's share some story time.
Come snuggle in here with me—
now doesn't this feel fine?

When I was just a boy, about the size of you,
I loved to cuddle in my bed and dream as now I do
'bout all the things I wished would be and all the things that are,
from Big Rock Candy Mountain to sparkles of a star.
Yes, bedtime was my favorite. 'Twas my time only then
to think of what the morn would bring and all that just had been.
I dreamed of Mom and Daddy and all my school-time chums.
I dreamed of grass and hilltops, of cake and bubble gum.
See, drifting into Dreamland's like floating on a raft—
it's sometimes slow and lazy; it sometimes rushes past.
What really makes it super, a fun, exciting scene,
no matter what you dream of, no matter where you've been,
you'll always know I love you. Remember what I've said—
you wake and I'll be near you to hear what's in your head.
So dream, my fine young buddy, and if you're so inclined,
I'd love to share tomorrow the treasures of your mind.

First printed in
Rainbows, Butterflies and Other Assorted Edibles

Mr. Whimsy

CINQUAINS

Cinquains:
five line poems
with two syllables in
the first, then four, six, eight and two.
Like this.

Sitting
'neath the sun one
day, I thought I'd capture
it succinctly in the form of
cinquains:

New sun,
climbing the sky,
stretching, reaching, calling
out to tell the world, "It's time to
wake up."

Child-like.
That's what you are
as you play hide-and-seek
in a blue sky full of fluffy
white clouds.

So hot
you make people
dance on the sand, while you
unabashedly do a jig
at sea.

Who Put the "P" in Pneumonia?

Cruel sun,
singeing my skin,
spearing my eyes with glare,
sucking liquid from me until
I crack.

I like
you best, Sir Sun,
playing in the sprinklers,
turning each water drop into
a pearl.

Pale light.
Hard, slanting sky.
What's the matter, Sir Sun?
You look as though you've seen
a ghost.

Putting
yourself to bed,
you sigh orange, wink scarlet,
then pull the dark blanket over
your head.

Mr. Whimsy

CAIRO

A scrunched up sheet of paper
is an everlasting joy.
Most anything he looks at
he converts into a toy.
He is active and so agile.
He is *CURIOSITY*.
The entire world's his oyster.
He's as playful as can be.
He's a never-ending whirlwind.
He's an acrobat and pryer.
He can jump and climb and stalk and bend,
but never is a crier.
The strangest things he plays with—
almost any you can mention.
The only thing he's lacking
is the span of his attention.
If human, he would giggle;
he would laugh and shriek and shout.
Then, suddenly in Dreamland,
he would smile, as he conked out.
He constantly is happy.
He never gives us sass;
and lands in crazy places
after running out of gas.
Adorable. Amusing.
With him we're truly smitten.
I thought I'd introduce to you
our eight-week-old Mau kitten.

Who Put the "P" in Pneumonia?

THE CAT AND THE PRINTER

Our cat is enthralled with our printer.
I'm somewhat amazed in that
it prints, and he's there! What a sprinter!
He must be a *copy cat.*

Mr. Whimsy

                                                  r
                                                  e
Chasing rainbows,   a
                                               l
        I oft times run into   i
                                               t
                                               y

The bump startles me,

but in an odd way it

                     feels good.

First printed in
Rainbows, Butterflies and Other Assorted Edibles

Who Put the "P" in Pneumonia?

CHEEK SCAR

A cattle wrangler years ago,
I sat at the campfire sippin' joe.
A coyote out to find her pup
by nosin' 'round got the herd stirred up.
That weren't too bad but then, ya see,
a cougar showed. Weighed two times me.
Some dumb cowpoke shot off his gun.
Them skittish cows began to run.
They headed my way. My horse broke loose
and stomped on me; that durn cayuse.
His reins hung low. And bein' bold,
I reached right out and grabbed ahold.
He yanked his head. I held that tack
and soon wound up on my stallion's back.
So what if his hoof had met my face;
it mighta hurt more in another place.
We turned that herd. It was tough to move it.
I've got the scar on my cheek to prove it.

Written to commemorate a basal cancer removal.

Mr. Whimsy

FEAR NOT

When to loving heights you soar
with the one whom you adore,
feel and fly. Fear not. Explore!
That's what *passion nets* are for.

Who Put the "P" in Pneumonia?

FISH 'N MAN

A man reeled in a good-sized fish—
so big that folks along the shore
came from far to stare at it;
a few at first, then many more.
While down the beach a little way
a carp pulled in a fishing man
attracting from the nearest school
a very finny, fishy clan.
Said the fisherman with mustered glee,
"I'm truly happy as can be.
I'd love to swap fish tales, you bet,
but do believe I'm much too wet!"
To which the fishes did reply,
"Our friend on land is much too dry.
We'll let you go, if you behave
and send him in on the next big wave."

Mr. Whimsy

THE FIVE-SECOND LAG

At times I feel I've lost my mind,
at least, left some of it behind.
The memory portion is what lags.
Five seconds after me it tags.
I find my speech I interrupt
while waiting for it to catch up.
It's usually just a single word.
Forgetting it seems quite absurd.
Then summoned by an unheard gong
that word comes ambling along,
completing what I had in mind
but for a short time couldn't find.
When I tell friends what I go through
they simply say, "What else is new!"
It seems it happens to them too,
not one or two, but quite a few.
Such mystery I cannot unfold.
It couldn't be I'm "getting old"!
Now, this solution may sound dumb
but… Wait five seconds. It will come.

Who Put the "P" in Pneumonia?

FIVE-YEAR-OLD LOVE

"Billy. Oh, Billy,
I love you so much!"
his smiling mama said.
"How much do you love me?"
he wanted to know,
a measuring stick in his head.
"This much, no,
T — H — I — S much," his mama replied,
spreading her arms open wide.
"Mommy, you know
how much I love you?"
tiny Billy then cried.
His answer brought tears
to his mama's eyes,
for little Bill didn't dally,
"All the way to Moore's market
and back.
And that's not taking the alley!"

Mr. Whimsy

FLOATER IN MY EYE

I have a fair-sized floater
that travels in my eye.
It did appear quite suddenly
and will not say bye-bye.
I took it to the doctor, a retinologist,
who couldn't find the slightest tear,
although the lines persist.
There's neither flash nor checkered flag.
It's just a squiggly line
that dances in the corner
on a vertical incline.
It does enhance my vision
with occasional design.
But doctors, we all know, are right,
so all should be just fine.

Who Put the "P" in Pneumonia?

FOLKS WOULD SAY

If I could dance a chocolate waltz
or sing a candy song,
folks would say, "He's really sweet."
And they would not be wrong.
If muscle bubbles I could blow,
now that would be a sight!
Folks would say, "His breath is strong."
They would, of course, be right.
If I could sigh geraniums
or chat in pansies blue,
they'd say my speech is flowery.
And that would be quite true.
If I could live in outer space
and twink my smile afar,
so brilliant I'd be called by all;
yes, I could be a star.
And, if I whistled blizzard tunes
or icicles could drool,
they might shiver when I pass,
but folks would say, "He's cool."
Not one of these things can I do.
I am no kind of whiz.
But I'm sure pleased when people say,
"He's loved for what he is."

Mr. Whimsy

FORCED-AIR HEATING

I've searched all over,
high and low,
for more than heated air.
I've whined, I've pined,
but cannot find
those *four stairs* anywhere!

Who Put the "P" in Pneumonia?

FRECKLE COLLECTOR

A freckle collector! A freckle collector!
I see by your skin you're a freckle collector.
Can't tell what you're thinking.
Can't tell where you've been.
But your passion for freckles is plain as your skin.
You say you don't like them? They don't make you grin?
Oh, come now, my dear one, you'd best think again,
for a freckle trail's magic wherever it goes—
across your shoulders or over your nose,
down your forearms, around your knees,
freckles are free to roam as they please.
But, oh, when they find that place they like best,
better than any and all the rest,
they stake their claims; they mark their spots
with various shades in the shape of dots.
Then we can all tell. And we should all care
that something quite special and loved is right there.

Mr. Whimsy

INTRIGUING YOU ARE

Intriguing you are
as the first-sighted star
on a balmy, moonlit eve.
You hold my attention
yet cause much dissention
on whether to rejoice or grieve;
for, like a lone sprite,
you stand out so bright
from your sandy surroundings that sprawl.
You're a sparkling straight pin.
And the trouble I'm in
is that I am a rubber beach ball.

First printed in
Rainbows, Butterflies and Other Assorted Edibles

I THINK I'M IN LOVE WITH YOU

I think I'm in love with you.

Well, maybe not quite yet. We've known each other only 45 minutes. But the possibility is 99 percent.

I can already feel what it will be like. My fall will definitely be head first. Yep, head-over-heels.

You're amazingly attractive. Not only on the outside. Your poise and gracious manner gently emanate from your soul. They bathe others with soft rays of enchantment. I understand the contentment those rays bring to people. It's pleasant waiting to see and hear what comes next.

You radiate delight. Effuse wonder. Elicit dreams. All without trying to do so.

You're an absolute find. A blind-date-miracle.

I'm thoroughly enjoying each second I'm with you. I've no time for expectations. I can't afford to miss a moment of the present.

Your charms bring marvels to life and make them accessible. With a deep breath, I realize I never before knew how a flower feels when it blooms. Then, I met you.

Sitting back, inhaling perspective, I realize how fortunate I am to meet you at this stage of my life. I'm free, experienced and appreciative.

What an unexpected privilege. A magnificent coincidence. But I don't believe in coincidences.

There's a reason for our meeting. It's that one day I will have the extreme pleasure of hearing you whisper in my ear, "I think I'm in love with you."

Mr. Whimsy

RESPONDING TO A COMPLIMENT
ON ONE OF MY WRITINGS

"Thank goodness these things
just come through me.
If I had to think them up on my own,
I'd be in deep trouble."

Who Put the "P" in Pneumonia?

I'LL LOAN YOU MY WHISPER

I'll loan you my whisper
but would like it back.
It has all these neat things to say
like, "Sweet dreams, my Darling,"
and "I love you so,
Tomorrow will be a great day."
For now, though, you have it
all tucked in your ear
to hear when you're nestled in bed;
so go brush your "toofers"
and wash your face well
and comb the blond hair on your head.
Then under the covers;
now off goes the light;
just settle on down with a sigh.
You'll have my soft whisper.
Do listen to it;
and know that your Daddy's close by.

First printed in *Strawberry Glue*

Mr. Whimsy

GROWING AND CHANGING

My furry caterpillar became a butterfly.
My tadpole went and changed into a toad.
The little fib I made up turned out to be a lie.
The path I started down became a road.
Things are changing daily, at least that's what I'm told.
I guess I'm getting big enough to care.
I'm far from being grown enough to be considered old,
but now each day I change my underwear.

Who Put the "P" in Pneumonia?

MY GRANNY RIDES A HARLEY

My Granny rides a Harley.
My Granny bungie jumps.
My Granny is a skier.
My Granny takes her lumps.
My Granny likes to SCUBA.
My Granny sky dives too.
My Granny's into surfing.
Can all these things be true?
My Granny's been bucked from a bronco.
My Granny's swung on a trapeze.
My Granny's led jungle safaris
and hung from a plane by her knees.
What other activities Granny
is into I only can guess
for when they are shown on our TV,
excitedly Granny cries, "YESSSSS!"
My Granny's mind's open and willing.
Her body is healthy it seems.
My Granny's life's very exciting,
but mostly, I think, in her dreams.

Mr. Whimsy

GROWING VOCABULARY

My vocabulary's growing.
It is filling up my mind
with so many words and phrases
of a new and different kind.
There are "cyber vandals hacking,"
"sky-boarders shredding air"
which are action-linked attractions
that not long ago weren't there.
It is fun and quite exciting
for it stimulates my brain
and permits my coining phrases
while not being called insane.

HE BE JEEBEE

I was scalped by a hair-hoarding jeebee!
He commenced in the midst of the night.
He was only half done when I wakened.
I brushed him away in a fright!
He had started up front on my forehead—
'bove my eyebrows he'd made his first slice.
He had peeled my hair back in his gentle attack,
when I shouted "THAT'S NOT VERY NICE!"
He asked could he keep what he'd started.
I uttered, "Okay, but now GO!"
He whispered these words as we parted,
"You're really quite different, you know;
for most people snooze through the scalping.
They feel not molested, nor mauled.
They sleep through each night nonchalantly;
then one day they reckon they're bald."
I peered in the eyes of the jeebee.
He seemed quite sincere, yet intense.
He left without telling who he be.
I've not seen my forehead hair since.

Mr. Whimsy

I'M STANDING IN THE CORNER

I'm standing in the corner with my nose against the wall.
It's not that plaster smells good. No, it's just so I won't fall.
You see, it gives me balance, for I have no spine at all.
Life's awkward for a noodle which is nearly ten feet tall.
I used to be more sturdy until I slipped in oil
and fell into a geyser where I began to boil.
I managed to escape it by clinging to some soil.
But fast enough I wasn't. My firmness seemed to spoil.
The broccoli and carrots enjoyed such a dip.
Although they blanched initially, they kept stiff upper lips.
But I'm becoming flimsy and fear that I will slip.
There's not much use for noodles when a noodle's lost its grip.

IMAGICATION

I now have my choice of the perfect vacation.
I'll conjure it up through imagination.
I'll do it while swimming for exercise;
while stroking, I'll calmly accept each surprise.
I'll start off by swimming the River of Duels
with banks made of gold and bed lined with jewels.
It's truly a treasure no other can see.
This vision so rich is seen only by me.
But, oh, what a wonder to start my vacation.
I now think I'll swim through a tasty libation
like salt margarita, a pina colada,
or one I've created, a mango tangada.
I'll swim up the Matterhorn, ski down its slope.
Then maybe I'll glide through a kaleidoscope.
Post landing I'll graze at a buffet profound—
hors d'oeurves and desserts without gaining a pound.
But first I will swim to the African plains
to race a sleek cheetah and comb some lion manes.
To Rome I'll next stroke to coin Trevi fountain;
and then off to Rio's small Sugarloaf mountain.
A good game of golf I now wish to play.
I'll picture each shot as I swim on my way;
then dive nearby tropics to view brilliant fish
and up through the sky on a star-studded swish.
That's how I've done it. I'm nobody's fool.
I've travelled the world without leaving the pool.

Mr. Whimsy

THE INVISIBLE BOGEY MAN

The invisible bogey man—
I can *see* him. I swear that I can!
He is right over there
just behind the stuffed chair.
Now he's jumped to the stair!
He's as big as a bear!
He's got rattlesnake hair!
And his eyes spark and glare!
So I must be aware
that if I meet his stare,
I will fry in mid-air!
I won't LOOK! I don't DARE.
Oh, my gosh! What a scare!
How I wish he weren't there.
I can't GO anywhere!
And that's really NOT keen
'cause tonight's Halloween!

Who Put the "P" in Pneumonia?

IT IS BECOMING COMMONPLACE

You live your life in cyberspace
and, yet, you neither rush nor race.
In fact you manage from one place
with style. I'd even say with *grace*.
It is your home, your work, your base
from which most matters you can trace
and solve what problems you may face.
I must, indeed, give up the chase
and slow my frantic, hectic pace.
I drive to malls; my shoes I lace;
I carry extra pens "in case"
and manually mistakes erase.
Yes, it's becoming commonplace.
This *cyberspace* I must embrace.

Mr. Whimsy

MIND MEADOW

My mind meadow is where I go
when I'm ready to sleep at night—
a place that's fun and full of sun
where everything's all right.
I lie here in the lush green grass.
I hear the brook and bees.
I feel the warmth upon my back
'midst aromatic breeze.
It usually takes a breath or two
and then I'm all at ease,
and have sweet dreams
the whole night through
with images like these:
Rabbits white and butterflies,
blue birds and balloons;
foxy friends and friendly words
and chests of gold doubloons.
Jungle scenes with tiger stripes;
flamingos in a pool;
mangoes juicy, soft & ripe
and glens of shady cool.
Velvet sighs and lullabies
and back scratches galore,
and all that's pleasant from the past
and all good things in store.

Who Put the "P" in Pneumonia?

RABBIT HOLE

I've gone to my Mind Meadow for good
and down the rabbit hole
where warm, white light improves my sight
and polishes my soul.
The walls of the hole are soft, yet firm;
they help me shed my skin.
The way is tight but mellow bright.
I seem to flow right in.
I'm now composed of pure white air
and like a magnet drawn
up and onward, who knows where,
toward a dazzling dawn.
I have no cares. I'm joyous, whole.
I'm here. I'm everywhere—
a carefree, weightless, happy soul
that now needs no repair.
I've melded with the universe.
In tune. In harmony.
And all there is
is all I am
as far as I would be.

Mr. Whimsy

IT'S ALMOST TIME

No wonder his skin's scales abound
and eyes are full of tears—
the crocodile has hung around
200 million years!
His smiling mouth reflects his thought—
he conjures dreams of dating.
But how much longer has he got?
He's done a lot of waiting.
His calm and patient nature shows;
his store of wisdom's great.
Those tears are happy ones. He knows
she's always *somewhat* late.

Who Put the "P" in Pneumonia?

JANUARY SECOND

Gymnasiums are busting at their seams,
full of folks with slimness in their dreams.
But two weeks from today
they'll all have gone away
- to once again eat candy and ice creams.
- with broken wills and tattered self-esteems.
- with much distain for trying new regimes.

Mr. Whimsy

KIND SISTERS

Karen and Sharon were two of a kind.
Their actions, however, gave pause to my mind.
When Karen was sharin', I was amused.
Then Sharon was carin' and I was confused.

JUST ONE BOOK

If on a desert island I were stranded
and had my choice of but one book to read,
(a tome through which my life could be expanded)
there is a certain one I'd choose, indeed!
It wouldn't be the Bible, although that book is "Good".
It would not be the longest I could find.
It would not be a novel, although, of course, it could.
This book's each page invigorates my mind—
a book of many subjects, whichever I would choose.
No, an encyclopedia it's not.
It never fails to fascinate whenever I peruse,
although it has no frothy, detailed plot.
It offers both tranquility and mighty mutablility.
It is a book of which I would not tire.
It's graced with broad utility as well as the ability
to stimulate my authoring desire.
I'd want no large anthology, nor study of astrology;
and, yet, this book contains both "star" and "verse."
It surely is no mystery, not even based on history,
though curiously, even more diverse.
So what will last a lifetime and always bring me bliss?
I've hinted I am somewhat fiction-wary.
Of all the vast selection, my choice is clearly this—
a wondrous, word-chocked, great, thick dictionary.

Mr. Whimsy

LICENSES

A driver's license allows you to drive;
a fishing license, to fish.
"Poetic license" allows you to do
with words whatever you wish.
You can use poor grammar
like "me" for "I".
You can misstate tenses of time.
You can do things absurd
like creating a word
in order to make a verse rhyme.

Who Put the "P" in Pneumonia?

LIFE IS FULL OF MYSTERIES

Life is full of mysteries,
not all things what they seem.
But the names we give to many
are really not that keen.
Think with me now as I explore
some very subtle lies;
they deal with names we've given
to varieties of flies—
a horsefly cannot speak, of course,
so do we know that it is hoarse?
A dragonfly is much too small
to drag much anything at all.
Why do we call them butterflies,
when what they do is flutter by?
See what I mean? It's strange, indeed.
But here's the total "ripper"—
the fly we're most familiar with
is one that's called "the zipper!"

First printed in
Rainbows, Butterflies and Other Assorted Edibles

Mr. Whimsy

LIGHT SAVERS

Bobby's finding bottles!
Janet's hunting jars!
We'll set them where the sun shines,
like on the tops of cars.
When they're full of sunbeams
we'll screw the lids on tight
so none that we've collected
can fly away at night.
We may be one day early
but, golly, that's no crime.
We just heard—tomorrow
starts Daylight-Savings-Time!

Who Put the "P" in Pneumonia?

LOOK UP

Huge toothless dragons with bows on their tails.
Sleek submarines that balloon into whales.
Castles and poodles, piglets and apes—
constant displays in a world changing shapes.
Snowmen on horseback chase buffalo herds.
Slow-mo explosions, which charm beyond words.
Where do they come from and where do they go?
Who cares, my friend, let's enjoy the show.
No need for tickets. Admission is free.
Open the eyes of your mind and you'll see
magical worlds of shapes which do please
filling the skies o'er Caribbean seas.

Mr. Whimsy

SHORELINE

The waves roll in. The waves retreat,
erasing prints of tiny feet
of searching birds and kids at play,
who then reprint them right away.

LOST HEAD

I woke up this mornin' and my head fell off.
What made it even worse, I was sleepin' in the loft.
It thumped down the ladder, was kicked by a cow.
You better believe that hurt. And how!
I reached for my comb to fix my hair
then realized that my head weren't there.
Is this what they mean whene'r it's said
"It just ain't cool to lose your head?"
My nose could smell; my eyes still see.
My ears could hear, but they weren't with me.
Just where they were was hard to tell,
'cause my head lurched on pell-mell for a spell.
It pitched down the dell, then bounced in the well.
Yep, into the deep, dark depth it fell.
A *SPLASH* it made and when it rose
my mouth called out to my feet and toes,
which ran to the well. That ain't too shoddy.
But they left so fast, they forgot my body!
So here I lie (just a little bit).
It's more of a spoof than a counterfeit.
It may be bad, but it ain't the worst,
'cause I'm just a-foolin'. It's April 1st!

Mr. Whimsy

My wife returned from her mother's home carrying a white paper bag, which she placed on our dining room table. I later found her sitting at the table. She had emptied the contents of the bag to form a pile of small cylindrical objects wrapped in faded newspaper. She explained they were crystals from her grandmother's chandelier.

While she gazed at the pile, as if she could see through the paper into another world, I gently slipped a memory disc from her mind into my imagination player to create:

MY GRANDMOTHER'S CHANDELIER

My grandmother's chandelier…
(my grandmother's chandelier)—
what a glorious sight as we'd gaze through the night
at my grandmother's chandelier.
My grandmother's chandelier
was once more than it now may appear—
it would sparkle and glint (even more, if we'd squint)
as we conjured up dreams so clear.
You see, we respected that she had collected
the crystals from many a land.
And the stories she told, be they tender or bold,
had helped us to understand
why each crystal tear she did so revere,
for each had a tale of its own.
Yes, the joy we'd share as we lingered there
was the warmest I'd ever known.
Of castles we learned, of romances spurned,
of statesman and gondolier.
Our vision flew far as if led by a star
in our grandmother's chandelier.

Who Put the "P" in Pneumonia?

We sipped heady wine, viewed dancers divine,
were enthralled by the atmosphere
of flamboyance and grace, which had once taken place
'neath our grandmother's chandelier.
Now the lady is gone but the magic hangs on
in the mystical crystals so dear.
And the loved narratives continue to live
in my grandmother's chandelier.
That was long, long ago but is still true I know,
so pardon me, please, if I peer
for a few moments more and enjoy the lore
of my grandmother's chandelier.

Mr. Whimsy

LUNCH IN THE SHADE OF THE SLURP-N-BURP TREE

Just you and me and the Slurp-n-Burp tree
a-sittin' here, you know.
Makes me wonder 'bout some things
like where'd the others go?
Where's Jim and Jack and Joe and Mack
and Jane and Pete and Jerry?
And George and Sue and Jake and Lou
and Skip and Sam and Terri?
We were a bunch;
then all through lunch
I heard a kind of SLURP.
And then a crunch,
a muffled munch,
a swallow and a burp …
(SLURP, CRUNCH, munch, BURP)
I'm starting to get a bit nervous.
'Cause now, you see,
there's only ME
a-sittin' here 'neath the Slurp-n-Burp tree!

Who Put the "P" in Pneumonia?

MANDRILL
(baboon)

The mandrill is amazing-faced.
With colored patterns it is graced.
Yet, by this question some are stumped:
Why IS the mandrill brightly-rumped?
A make-up artist he must be
to paint his face so prettily.
But organized this creature ain't,
for then he sits down in the paint!

Mr. Whimsy

MARSHA

Marsha's white and, some say, "plushy",
but she changes in the heat—
she gets soft and somewhat mushy.
Yet, she's always very sweet.
"Pliant…Gooshy!" some folks bellow,
"More like gooey than like jello!"
"Phooey!" finally says one fellow,
"Marsha's simply very mellow!"

Who Put the "P" in Pneumonia?

MEDICAL TESTS

I feel good. But maybe I shouldn't.
I've learned from my doctors, things that I wouldn't
believe or think are wrong with me.
I feel as healthy as can be.
But one test leads to another, and then
instead of one thing wrong, there's ten.
I've come to believe it's unjust aggravation.
The "cascade" has grown to a "constellation."
These terms are fun till I think about it.
But scheduled openings make me doubt it.
By openings I mean operations.
I guess they're more than aggravations.
But I don't hurt like you'd think I would.
Could it be that my attitude makes me feel good?

Mr. Whimsy

MY DOZEN COUSINS

Freddy wants his feet rubbed.
Betty needs her back scrubbed.
Charlie likes his chin chucked.
Thurman wants his thumb sucked.
Holly wants her hair combed.
Nellie needs her nose blown.
Toby wants his teeth brushed.
Eileen needs some ice crushed.
Gabby wants to go shop.
Kenny needs a cough drop.
Stanley wants a steak fried.
Hanna wants her hands dried.
And me, poor me, I've really tried.
I've tried and tried and tried and
T R I E D!
I've helped out this evening
and I am no quitter.
But next time, Dear Auntie,
PLEASE hire a sitter.

Who Put the "P" in Pneumonia?

NAMING THE PARROT

To Esther, the parrot, we'll add the name Polly.
She cannot eat carrots or crackers, by golly!
Now, if she were living, it would be pathetic.
But we, of course, know Polly Esther's synthetic.

Mr. Whimsy

NEW

It wasn't new to my wife. But it was new as could be to me.

Their relationship had evidently begun three months ago. I hadn't paid attention. Maybe that's why she wanted to be with him.

I'd been somewhat detached. I was busy, had things to accomplish.

I'd seen him before. A couple of times. He is definitely handsome. Young and buff. I figured he just worked the grounds inspecting various things.

One recent evening after calling out to my wife and receiving no answer, I searched the house. Couldn't find her.

Then I glanced outside into the dark patio. That's how I first found them together. He was black. I could hardly see him. As I watched more closely, it became obvious my wife and he were enjoying one another's company. They listened intently to each other, shared gentle touches.

I was surprised, actually shocked. There they were. Right on our property. But they were beautiful together. I found myself riveted by the scene. Entranced, yet torn emotionally. Why hadn't she told me about him?

Now here she is, openly fondling this wild handsome male. He looks lovingly at her and shivers in delight.

I remain silent. I've decided to let her tell me about him when she feels the time is appropriate.

Two nights later I step into our bedroom. I'm stunned. There she is. My beautiful blond wife on the settee with him. They're entwined. She strokes his sleek black body and whispers softly, "I love you, Louie."

I catch my breath. I feel a tinge of jealousy. Then my wife looks up at me and smiles, "Can we keep him?"

Louie just purrs.

NTH

A word without vowels. A rarity.
It's often used as "the nth degree."
It surely does seem strange to me
this truncated, stubby word can be
so closely aligned with infinity.
Is that just me? Or, do you agree?

Mr. Whimsy

CONVERSING WITH A NOSE

While talking to a nose today,
I've learned this organ cannot say
or hear what anything is all about.
Well, "anything" is rather broad.
In fact, its knowledge I applaud,
for to the sense of smell it is devout.
I'm not quite sure how it explained
the valued knowledge it obtained,
but somehow it did manage to disclose
the many subtleties of *smell*,
a subject that it's studied well.
About this sense the nose most surely knows—
there's the odor of a motor
that is recognized by boater
and the odor of a charming mademoiselle;
for it's not deemed *odor* should
be either bad of good.
No, *odor's* just another word for smell.
Now let's discuss *aroma*.
Unless you're in a coma,
you know that it is spicy and quite light.
On the other hand, *bouquet*,
the nose did seem to say,
refers to flowers or a wine that's right.
Both *fragrance* and *perfume*
you may, indeed, assume
pertain to flowers or to women's spray.
But you're truly getting warmer
if you understand the former
is more delicate in each and every way.
You may not know that *savor*
refers to smell or flavor.
And *scents* are fairly scattered through the air.

Who Put the "P" in Pneumonia?

Each aforementioned smell,
for the most part, treats us well.
The next, however's, quite beyond compare.
Yes, the *stench*—foul, strong, pervasive,
is so rotten and persuasive
it creates an urge to leave. And you don't doubt it.
Just hope your nose plug fits,
for you can see that it's
superfluous to "raise a stink" about it.
Before the nose does run,
please come and join the fun
of choosing just which smell you like the best.
You're welcome to explore
with this proboscis, or
feel free to put your own nose to the test.

Mr. Whimsy

ODE TO A RHINOCEROS

You've grown a fine thorn.
So if you were petalled
and velvety-yellow with no great big nose;
had leaves and a stem
instead of thick haunches
and smelled sort mellow, you could be a rose.
But be as you are.
Your self is quite special.
You are unique and that you should stay.
I'll picture your rhinoness
knee-deep in roses.
Somehow the contrast has much more to say.

OFF WATERLEMON CAY

Off Waterlemon Cay
in luscious Leinster Bay
there lives a school of starfish
that's large in every way.
So many, many starfish
in every place you see
that one might even call them
a mini-galaxy.
Not only are there hundreds,
but each huge one I find
impresses me, possesses me,
makes me expand my mind.
It's very like a fairy tale
where stars fall from the skies
to grace the seas
with charm and ease
and wonderful surprise.

St. John, U.S. Virgin Islands

Mr. Whimsy

OH, MY DARLING

Oh, my darling,
my beloved,
without you
I can not endure.
I crave your lovely
shapely body
so tempting
yet divinely pure;
your eyes so dark,
your skin enchanting,
the tasteful jacket
that you wear;
it's too bad
you're a baked potato
and I am just
an unripe pear!

First printed in
Rainbows, Butterflies and Other Assorted Edibles

Who Put the "P" in Pneumonia?

ouch! Ouch! OUCH!

I'd just like to scream!
Too painful to pout.
No, nothing, it seems,
could be worse than the gout!

Mr. Whimsy

OLD SKIN
(for the grandkids)

I'm bringing my "old skin" to visit.
It is no longer firm, smooth and prime.
You can count all my scars and fine wrinkles.
We will have a most marvelous time.
There are many a nick, pock and cranny.
There are crevices deep to explore.
You may find spider veins, a few bowling lanes,
a wart, several moles and clogged pores.
Though it may not be handsome to look at,
here's a lesson which needs to sink in—
mine, at *one* time, was smooth as a peach's;
so be sure to take care of *your* skin!

Who Put the "P" in Pneumonia?

PATTY

Little Patty loved the sun,
standing 'neath it till she'd "run".
Rivulets of perspiration
became rivers of sweatation.
First, she was a waterfall;
then she was not there at all—
just a puddle on the floor.
Little Patty was no more.
Some say she was liberated.
I think she evaporated.
Wonder what she thought and felt
as she became a "patty melt."

Mr. Whimsy

THE PIRATE, M.T. FLAGON

I once was a pirate. In days of yore
I reveled in carnage, in guts and gore!
A ball from a cannon blew off me leg.
I had to make do with a wooden peg.
For practice with cutlass I struck the ship's mast;
that shattered me left hand—a thing of the past.
Yet, many a foe I did neatly dispatch
till a poke in me eye caused a need for a patch.
It covered me eye which was no longer there.
The word got around that me socket was bare.
When maties would ask could they sneak a short look,
I'd wave them away with me sharp, burnished hook.
Me parrot pal, Argh, on me shoulder would sit.
He loudly spewed words which were vile and unfit
except for the foulest of pirates to hear.
They smarted me eye! They shriveled me ear!
"Aaarrrgh!" I would shout, but he never did quit,
though his feathers would ruffle and quiver a bit.
I lost that low creature and earned me the name
of poor *M. T. Flagon.* The dice were to blame.

Yes, I was a pirate and that was my life,
but now I'm a poet with dear, loving wife.
That scoundrel, however, still lives deep within.
I keep him subdued and surrounded by skin.
I keep him benumbed in a piratey fog
by swilling occasional flagons of grog.
You question the long, jagged scar on my throat?
The trace of a dagger? A wild tale to quote?

Who Put the "P" in Pneumonia?

This marking is something I keep mum about.
It's the zipper that lets M.T. FLAGON COME OUT!!!
HAR! HAR! HAR! HAR! HAR!

Written to commemorate elective neck surgery.

Mr. Whimsy

RECIPE

Love.
Mix thoroughly
with life.
DO NOT DILUTE.

RecTangles

I refer to them as "tangles",
for they really are not "wrecked".
They retain their four right angles
though they're stretched to some effect.
They, in essence, are a sequel,
solid/strong. But be aware—
if their four sides still were equal,
they'd be known to us as "square".

Mr. Whimsy

RAINY DAY

Outside it's raining cats and dogs.
They're melting on the ground.
And I just bet because of this,
strange summer plants abound.
Come sit right here and think with me
how all will be surprised
by wondrous vegetation
that blooms before their eyes—
Tiger lilies and Dandelions,
Persian petunias and Ocelot vines,
Doberman daisies, hyacinth Hounds
and Beagle begonias all clustered in mounds;
Pekinese posies, Spaniel sweet peas,
Dalmatian dahlias and Terrier trees,
Collie chrysanthemums, Chihuahua chard,
Siamese sunflowers throughout the yard;
Tabby-like tulips, Basset hound beet,
Samoyed seedlings. Oh, what a treat!
They'll growl and purr and lick and bark.
And, should you search, when day grows dark,
all throughout these colorful tones
you'll find cat naps and lazy bones.

REFLEX

Said the nerve impulse to the brain one day,
"The stomach's hungry, but the hand can't stay
next to the food which the mouth will eat
for the food is sizzling in strong heat!
So what shall I tell the hand to do?"
The brain then thought the matter through
and quickly issued this command:
"Little Impulse, jerk the hand!
We, as a whole, will be a winner
 if the hand and mouth don't eat that dinner.
 The body will be just that much thinner.
 And no one will call us 'FATS

Mr. Whimsy

REMEMBER WHEN LAWMEN WERE HEROES? THEY STILL ARE

There was a time. Remember when?
I speak of yesteryear—
that "Hi, Ho, Silver!" brought a thrill
and Hoppy made us cheer.
The lawmen then were good guys.
They all were tried and true.
And *we* pretended we were *them*
in all that we would do.
The local cop was friend to all.
We'd wave to him and smile.
Our mothers introduced us kids
to officers worthwhile.
We'd seek them out if we were lost.
They solved our problems too.
We slept so soundly 'cause of them—
our heroes dressed in blue.
Well, they're the same. It's we who've changed.
They still serve and protect.
What they need now from all of us
is old fashioned respect.
And, though life's not as simple now,
we each can do our part.
Appreciating that they're there
is surely a good start.
Yes, we can let them know we care,
if you and I just save
a smile for every officer
accompanied by a wave.

Who Put the "P" in Pneumonia?

For smiles are quite contagious.
And waves aren't hard to give.
Combined they'll make a difference
in how we think and live.
There may be times they don't wave back.
But when one thinks, one finds
these days they have an awful lot
that occupies their minds.
So just imagine, if you will,
that 'fore their day is done,
they've mentally and from their hearts
returned to us each one.

Mr. Whimsy

RESTAURANT AQUARIUM

While I wait for "food to go",
fishes wander to and fro.
In the large aquarium
some do dart. Some slowly swim.
Most appear to feel just fine
as they watch me sip my wine.
Two of them I think are fighting
over what I might be writing.

Who Put the "P" in Pneumonia?

SMALL WONDER

Small wonder
which makes happiness abound—
the glance we share
when others are around.

First printed in
Rainbows, Butterflies and Other Assorted Edibles

Mr. Whimsy

ROOM IN MY HEART

Oh, Sweetheart, my Darling, so special to me,
my "wonderful daughter" you always will be.
Of course, I'm aware you are nearly full grown,
a woman on campus with life of your own.
But know deep within that we're never apart—
you always can visit the room in my heart.
This room, filled with love, is quite cozy, yet bright;
a place we can share during daytime or night.
Show up when it's sunny or cloudy outside;
at times you need comfort; are bursting with pride;
are thanking the heavens for gifts from above;
or when you, quite simply, just want to feel love.
The door's always open. You've no more to do
than silently enter. This room's just for you.
So give life your best; try tasting it all;
stretch well to your limits and do have a ball.
You're *so* very special as you now depart.
I can't wait to meet in the room in my heart.

Who Put the "P" in Pneumonia?

SHY, ROMANTIC LAKE

Tiny, smooching waves
nibbling and kissing the shoreline…
hesitating… retreating…
then coming back for more.

Mr. Whimsy

SCAR THROAT

My throat's where the pirate skewered me,
made me dance on the tip of his sword.
I did both the cha-cha and two-step
while the pirate just laughed. No, he roared!
My scar takes the form of a zigzag—
one "Z" 'neath another anew.
I'm thusly embossed 'cause I wriggled.
Now, I ask, "In my place, wouldn't you?"
You wonder how I came to be here?
Just how in the world I got free?
It took my intense concentration—
a straight *line of sight* I could see
from where on the deck I was "dancing"
to land, which was not far away.
I leapt on that line in an instant.
Once on it, I managed to stay.
My balance was good as I ran it.
That line held up fine in my mind.
Though the pirate continued to slash it,
he could slice only what was behind.
I kept that line steady before me.
It held very taut, firm and true.
And that, gentle friend's, how I'm able
to be here conversing with you!

Written to commemorate elective neck surgery.

Who Put the "P" in Pneumonia?

STEEPED DREAMS

"I dreamed I was a tea bag," she proclaimed as she awoke.
I knew not how to take it; as the truth or just a joke.
So, I brought her boiling water and much to my surprise
she popped from bed and jumped right in before my very eyes!
She lolled there for a minute, then dunked a time or two.
I must admit, no doubt of it, she made a right fine brew.

Mr. Whimsy

SECRET LANGUAGE

Let's make up a language only you and I can speak.
We'll practice till it's perfect. That should take about a week.
Rum stickita, bum stickita, he cat fat so rat
can mean, "I think you're special," and niceness things like that.
While *Jelly belly bazbo, rippo rappo sis boom bah*
means, "Can I play or spend the night? I'd better ask my ma."
Tick-o tock-o, lick-o lock-o, mick-o mock-o mood
means, " Sure, I'm kinda hungry, if you're gonna fix some food."
Loopity-loppity, lemony-jimmony, tippity-tappity toss?
means, "This is uncooked bacon that is topped with apple sauce?"
Wimbly-bimbly, whambly-bambly, whumbly-bumbly bees!
means, "Good spaghetti sandwich mixed with honey, clams and
              cheese!"
Mmmboy! Mmmjoy! Lippity lappity smacks
means "This is really neato! You are great at making snacks."
Hotty-potty, morum lotty, sweety tweety tease?
means *"*Will you pass the chili and more chocolate syrup, please?*"*
Sour-power, yum tum, gooey-fooey pot
means "Pickles dunked in gravy absolutely hit the spot!"
Gleepo-gloppo. Get the moppo; urpo-burpo ick!
means "Speaking all this secret stuff has made me sorta sick!"

Who Put the "P" in Pneumonia?

THE SCHWA

It's neither animal nor fowl.
It is, in fact, an unstressed vowel
which has no *long* nor *short* sound of its own.
It's so unstressed and so relaxed
it feels caressed and quite untaxed—
a mellow little fellow lacking tone.
It's unobtrusive, calm and mild;
so different from the macron wild
which causes vowels to sound so *long* or *hard*.
The breve, which makes vowels *soft* or *short*,
it cannot claim as close cohort
and gleans no special favor from the bard.
It truly is innocuous.
About it no one makes a fuss.
For one thing only, it deserves acclaim.
For that alone the schwa we'll cheer.
Yes, it is music to one's ear—
the suave, smooth-sounding stream that is its name.

The sound of a schwa is "uh'. The following are examples of schwas:
The "o" in love, the "a's" in America, the "ai" in mountain.

Mr. Whimsy

SEDONA

God had fun in Arizona.
It seems his playground was Sedona,
for there, with glee and twinkling eyes,
He made drip castles and mud pies
of red, red earth and mammoth size
and backed them up with azure skies.
Then on a whim, so there'd be change,
a weather show He did arrange.
It paints the land in patterns bold
through baking heat and clear, crisp cold.
It features puffy clouds of cream
and dark ones past which sun can beam;
incorporates amazing jolts
that take the form of lightening bolts!
Today, while visiting this place,
I feel a sense of awe and grace.
I catch my breath or simply stare
at "red rock beauty" everywhere.
And, as my wonder does abound,
I share the fun that God first found.
I thank you, God, this joyous day
for having taken time to play.

Who Put the "P" in Pneumonia?

SILHOUETTE

Two females
sit
facing
one another
heads nodded
intent
on what
transpires
between them—
a young mother
carefully
applying
first-time-polish
to the
gleeful fingernails
of her
tiny
daughter.

First printed in
Life Inside an Apostrophe

Mr. Whimsy

SHOWERING SHARON

My sis, Sharon, loves to shower
more than anyone I've seen.
She believes in water power;
feels it makes her squeaky clean.
Says the spray's like "liquid sunshine",
water drops are "honeyed dew".
Splatters patter out their own time
beating rhythms old and new.
She pretends she's in a forest
being drenched by waterfalls.
Then she's singing in a chorus
banging on the shower walls.
Lately she's been kind of quiet;
hasn't sung a single song.
No more raunchy, raucous riot.
Gee, I hope there's nothing wrong!

EEEEE YIPES!
The mirrors are fogged.
The drain is all clogged.
There's not a thing left but thick, heavy haze.
She's been so darn pelted
she just must have melted.
Why not? She's been *in there* for 33 days!

Who Put the "P" in Pneumonia?

SIMPLY AMAZING!

Dotty drives South. She's truly dyslexic.
Norman drives North with stomach that's peptic.
Fred follows Dotty, his mind on his job.
Right behind Norm drives full-bladder-Bob.
Speed demon Sam's had too much to drink.
Close he will keep behind Fred, he does think.
Ed's eighty-five with reflexes slow.
Bill's a bit blind but knows where to go.
Sid's on his cell discussing divorce,
following Bill who he thinks knows the course.
Long lines of speed in opposing directions
making miniscule driving corrections.
Simply amazing—they stay on their side.
One tiny error and they could collide.
No wall between them, but all will be fine
thanks to a flat, double-yellow, long line.

Mr. Whimsy

SOUNDS ALIKE

A *paring* knife to cut a *pear*?
They sound alike, but do I dare?
For, if I cut this fruit in two,
a *pair* of *halves* I'll *have for you*.
"*Four ewe*, indeed," the ram does bleat.
"*4…U*," the teacher does repeat.
It makes me think 'bout words I say
and wonder why *they're* (*their, there*)
spelled that *way* (*weigh, whey*)!

Who Put the "P" in Pneumonia?

SPARE TIME

I treat my spare time as a treasure.
It's really a great deal of fun.
I'm not playing golf for my pleasure.
I don't bike or lift weights or run.
I find that I don't do much drinking.
In fact, I need less food & sleep.
I've thoroughly stepped up my thinking.
My mind's taken one quantum leap.
By not doing all that I've mentioned,
you'd think that I'd feel "bad" or "worse".
But I keep enthused and "untensioned"
by creating volumes of verse.

The above makes me sound a bit physically meek;
but I manage to swim at least six days a week.
I select several verses with which I am smitten
and aquatically memorize what I have written.

Mr. Whimsy

SWAMPMOSS MOSE

Little Mose was born in the swamp
on a soft, green, mossy bed.
With snakes he swam. With rats he ran.
Got his hands bit off by a gater's head.
But that didn't bother Swampmoss Mose
'cause Swampmoss Mose had a set of toes
as fine as any man ever grows;
and with those toes, the whole swamp knows,
little Mose learned to count.
The frogs hopped by with her froglettes.
The fox ran by with her kits.
And Mose sat there with his toes in the air
havin' a ball countin' 'em all,
making sure everything fits.
Swampmoss Mose caught a fever.
His body became diseased.
They buried his toes in countable rows
and his rest wherever they pleased.

Who Put the "P" in Pneumonia?

STRAWBERRY JELLO

Late after dinner
I stroll by the refrigerator.
It throws open its door
and speaks to me in
strawberry jello.
It happys me.
I return to our living room
satisfied full
of jiggling smile.

Mr. Whimsy

SLEEPY GIANT

Many, many years ago, the daytime sky was blue as it is today. But the nighttime sky was milk-white instead of dark. The moon and stars were black as licorice.

Beneath this sky lived a young giant. He played in the countryside. He ate healthily—bushes and trees were his spinach and broccoli. He drank from ponds and cold mountain streams. He grew. And grew. And grew.

His only problem was the white sky at night. It was too bright to allow a good sleep. Though he ate like a teenager, he couldn't sleep like one. Lack of sleep bothered the giant. He became cranky and mean, sometimes tearing off the roof of a house to cover his face at night.

People feared the giant. They ran away from him. They trained their dogs to nip his toes.

The giant didn't like what was happening. He was a good person who no longer liked himself.

He needed sleep. But the night sky was always milk-white bright, while the stars looked like black freckles or scattered caviar eggs and the moon resembled a deep, dark hole.

One night, as the giant sat with his back against a mountain trying to feel better, an idea came to him. He jumped to his feet. He stretched his arm as far as he could reach, right into the black moon-hole.

He grabbed the inside of the hole and began pulling. He pulled and pulled. As he did, the dark came out with his hand. He pulled until he turned the nighttime inside out.

At last the sky was completely dark, the moon shined brilliantly and the stars twinkled like diamonds.

The giant slept long and deeply. When he awakened, he felt much, much better. He liked himself. And everyone else liked him too.

SUGGESTION

Think *slow-ly* about a big *yawn*…
how eas-y it is to pass on…
Just take a slight pause.
Now open your jaws…

See, there. It has just come and gone.

Mr. Whimsy

TANGLES, GRAM AND ZOID

It's true all rectangles
have four sides and right angles
with *two* of those sides shorter than the others.
So a parallelogram by the name of Slanted Sam
was not believed when he claimed they were brothers.
"You don't have the right angles,"
proclaimed the righteous tangles,
"you claim to be our brother but you can't!"
Replied the slanted gram, "I am the way I am."
He did not get upset nor rave or rant.
"I'm flexible, you see. It's a happy way to be.
I've learned to lean a bit one way or other.
My sides do not collapse. Like you, I'm strong. Perhaps
you now can understand that I'm your brother.
"Ah, yes, indeed, we see how siblings we could be!"
the tangles shared the thought they now enjoyed.
"You're one of us, Sam Gram. You surely are no sham.
And so is sister Tillie Trapezoid!"

Who Put the "P" in Pneumonia?

TASTE BUD TALK

"Bud, you've really got great taste!"
said a tongue cell to another.
"Thanks," the second said with haste,
"but you should see my brother.
I taste *salt*, but he tastes *sweet*,"
so he's a happy critter.
Yet, I suppose we're both a treat
compared to *sour* and *bitter*."

Mr. Whimsy

TECH WRECK

EMERGENCY! Computer crash! A very first for me.
Our regular computer man is… "Out of town? I see…"
But, luckily, our neighbor has a man who is first rate!
And he can be here speedily. Now that's what I call GREAT!
It truly is amazing. With all his bag of tricks,
this man's met a computer he cannot seem to fix!
Not only that, the new one, installed next by this jerk,
(the faster, better model) has features which won't work!
The thing that really burns me—I asked him 'fore he went,
"Is everything in ship-shape? Will it now *save* and *print*?"
Now something for my grandson I've typed and tried to save.
And, sure enough, this damn machine begins to misbehave.
It's not as if I'm asking for functions wild or great.
I simply want this stupid thing to save what I create.
I s'pose it goes to show me. On "tech" I can't depend.
If in my mind I log these poems, I'm better in the end.
But now it's one day later. The man's brought back our drive.
He has retrieved most info to keep its soul alive.
To me he has explained things. They do not sound absurd.
I'll try hard to remember, but I'm no computer nerd.

THANKSGIVING DAY

So much there is to be thankful for—
so many a feeling and friend.
Yes, life's overflowing with things to adore.
Indeed, it appears there's no end.
Appreciating is truly a joy.
There's love everywhere that I look.
And lucky for me (Oh, boy! Oh, boy!)
my wife is a fabulous cook!

Mr. Whimsy

TICKLEBUG

The Ticklebug's coming
with fingers so long.
It's smiling and singing
the Ticklebug song:
"Tickle-dee, tickle-dee,
tickle-dee-dee,
I'll tickle your ribs.
I'll tickle your knee.
I'll tickle your tootsies.
And then, what the heck,
I'll blow 'gainst your skin
on the side of your neck!
You'll laugh and you'll giggle.
You'll twist and you'll wiggle.
You'll barely be able to breathe.
But that's when I'll cease.
I'll give you some peace.
You'll have what is called a 'reprieve'.
We will then sit and chat.
Or we might pet the cat
till your tiny smile grows to a grin.
Then my fingers unfold,
become tickle-dee bold,
and… we… start up all over again!"

TREMOR

It seems I've developed a tremor,
so a slight change in "drink plans" I'm makin'.
Martinis will still be my preference,
but, henceforth, never stirred, always shaken!

Mr. Whimsy

TODAY I FOUND YOU WAITING

Today I found you waiting—
just basking in the sun,
hoping I would pick you up,
take you and have some fun.
You looked a little strange to me,
yet quite familiar too.
I wasn't sure where you belonged
or just what I should do.
But seeing no harm in it
and being just a male,
I carefully surveyed you.
Yes, eyeing head and tail.
Though there are many like you,
my joy does abound.
You differ from all others
'cause you're the one I found.
Your worth to me is special,
I'll no longer run amok.
You're a sparkling, shiny penny
and you're going to bring me luck.

Who Put the "P" in Pneumonia?

TROPICAL TASTE TREAT

Today I turned the tables—it's super tasty neato!
I found that I was able to eat a few mosquitos.
It's best if you can catch them flitting through the air.
It's not too hard to snatch them. They're almost everywhere.
I actually prefer them with drops of sauces hot;
in quantity, as burgers; but that takes quite a lot.
So when those creatures tiny, charge forth in an attack,
don't flinch or just act whiney. Stand firm and bite 'em back!

Mr. Whimsy

TRISKAIDEKAPHOBIA
(fear of the number 13)

I hear that in Monrovia
there's triskaidekaphobia
and no one knows exactly how to cure it.
You cannot simply take a pill
or get a shot or pay a bill
to make it go away and then ensure it.
You don't know what comes ova ya
when triskaidekaphobia
slips slowly 'round your soul and makes you fear
the number, thirteen; nothing more;
not ghosts nor goblins, ghouls nor gore,
just one and three together. It's quite queer.
My name is Del Arobia
and triskaidekaphobia
has no effect on me that I have seen.
I even feel the number's luck
will soon help me to make a buck,
for I was born on Friday, 4/13.
So I'll go to Monrovia
where triskaidekaphobia
is running wild and causing people grief.
I have a plan which I've worked out.
When I reveal what it's about,
why, it will bring the populace relief.
You see, the trick is just to find
whatever takes the thought from mind
and keeps it out forever down the line.
I've tried it 12 times in the past
and each one's better that the last.
So number 14 ought to work out fine!

Who Put the "P" in Pneumonia?

THE TWO IMPOSTORS

The two impostors, Time and Space,
set out to run a foolish race—
"How fast one travels is the key!"
"How far one goes means more to me!"
And as they argue forth and back
I've come to see they both do lack;
for I can travel, I do find,
as fast or far as can my mind.
To Time and Space I've naught to prove.
I beat them both without a move.

Mr. Whimsy

UNDERSTANDING UMPS

I do understand why camels have humps.
I've figured out, too, why washboards have bumps.
I've counted the corners on cubed sugar lumps.
I've heard that in "bridge" there are card plays called "trumps".
I've saved lots of breath using bicycle pumps.
I cheer when poor players break out of their slumps.
I love throwing dirt clods I pull up in clumps.
I try not to call people frumps, grumps or chumps.
I know how some tree trunks are turned into stumps,
but still have to learn about glumps, yumps, and zumps.
Right now I'm a little bit down in the dumps—
my brand new bike's LONESOME. What causes the mumps?

Who Put the "P" in Pneumonia?

THE WARTHOG

"Ugly" is a state of mind,
for in the warthog I do find
such a strong and handsome brute
with razor-tusked, wide lumpy snoot;
stocky shoulders, legs so thin,
a scraggly mane and short-haired skin.
About its looks I have no qualm.
Of course, I am the warthog's mom.

Mr. Whimsy

UNPLANNED

What started as a small, green growth
    has now become a stalk.
        It also is the subject of
            our neighbors' nervous talk.
              This magical, expanding plant
            has grown above our fence.
        Its foliage, which once was scant,
has now become quite dense.
 It climbs and curls. It twists and turns
      while sprouting leaves which look like ferns.
        It wiggles, squiggles, stretches, blooms
           and grows through windows, filling rooms.
          The furniture it now entwines.
              It fondles fixtures with its vines.
          It turns on faucets, flicks each light.
          It wraps 'round pets and holds them tight.
       It slithers hither, thither, yon.
     It will not rest. It presses on.
      I swear I heard it squeal and cheer
          while lacing through our chandelier.
         Resembling an alligator,
             it's raiding our refrigerator!
              And now. Oh, gosh, I may be ill—
            it snakes through toilet bowls at will!
          It's shooting up the chimney flue!
      Oh, what am I supposed to DO?
     I fertilized and soaked
       the garden; but I must
         truly beg your pardon,
         for, one thing I
         forgot, indeed —
        I never pulled
        a single weed.

Who Put the "P" in Pneumonia?

WHAT ONCE WAS WHITE

What once was white is turning bare.
It's quite a fright. No longer there!
It's not Alaskan snow in May,
but my own hair. I'm sad to say.

Mr. Whimsy

WHAT'S THE GREEN IN OUR GARAGE?

What's the green in our garage
oozing under the door?
I've never seen green glow like that.
Well, maybe once before
But that I put out of my mind
to think about no more.
I've seen green trees and green neckties.
I've seen green thumbs and jealous eyes.
I've seen green gills, green apple pies.
But WHAT'S that under the door?
Green's just a mixture of yellow and blue.
I know that and so do you.
Good grief! It's getting on my shoe!
What IS that under the door?
Be calm. What's green and tends to sooth?
Landscapes hanging in the Louvre?
What the heck. I think I'll move!
Who cares what's under the door!

IF WE COULD VIBRATE

If we could vibrate at a much higher rate,
I wonder just how life would be.
Would there be need to touch, to see, hear and such,
at least as we do currently?
I imagine we'd feel with electronic zeal
and could see without using our eyes.
We could communicate in a manner first rate
without speaking. But that's no surprise.
We'd be well-tuned to all, be they grown or quite small,
whether near or in far distant place.
Life would be pleasant. No future, past, present.
There'd no longer be *time* and *space*.
Not one would have need for envy or greed;
we'd have access to all any time—
an endless supply of whatever we'd try,
our wishes fulfilled and sublime.
Our only desire would be to inspire
immersion in love's gentle glow—
a subtle vibration, a soft celebration
of all we are privileged to know.
How sweet it does sound where bliss does abound.
Such marvelous manifestations!
But I think I'll wait, not anticipate,
and revel in *this* world's sensations.

Mr. Whimsy

FURD

The strangest creature I ever saw
is the swivel-hipped, six-eyed Kinkajaw.
He opens his mouth to deliver a word
and his jaw kinks up, so he sounds absurd.
He rolls five eyes and he winks with one
then he wiggles his hips and he swivels 'em some.
He'll laugh and holler and giggle and spit
and massage his jaw till it creaks a bit.
Then he licks his chops, takes a bite of Furd …
"Furd?" you ask. "Just what is Furd?"
There's lots of thoughts, but the best I've heard
is Furd's the stuff that by Nature's law
can unkink the kink of a Kinkajaw.

Who Put the "P" in Pneumonia?

MOON BEAMING

My moon trip just the other night
was so much fun and such a sight!
There were no clouds. So clear it gleamed.
The moon reached down. It softly beamed
and smiling, took me up so fast,
I reveled in the ray it cast.
It takes no time at all it seems
when travelling forth and back on beams.
Yes, going up was like a breeze—
I *thought* my way; advanced with ease.
At first, I doubted getting back—
the moonbeam made a wider track.
So much of Earth it lit so bright,
it startled me; gave me a fright.
Within that space I couldn't find
my house by sight! I'd use my *mind*—
the path shown clear within my head.
I slid right down it into bed!

Mr. Whimsy

ZAMBOANGA

Zamboanga…what a name!
I know not what this place can claim—
a swaying palm, a striped sunset?
I'd check it out on the internet
but, actually, would rather dream
that all therein is life supreme.
In fact, I do not wish to know
if it's a country ravaged; so
I'll neither hunt nor nose around.
I'll simply let its mellow sound
carry me to worlds unknown
and leave the internet alone.

I eventually went to the internet
and discovered there to my regret
that it's no land of idyllic scenes,
but a *city* within the Philippines;
which goes to show, as I've often said,
Life's more beautiful inside my head!

Who Put the "P" in Pneumonia?

BAT WING STEW
(with firey dragon spice)

I love bat wing stew
with a frog's eye or two
and a handful of green lizard tails;
some cackles and chuckles,
encrusted chimp knuckles
and squoosh-gooshy, shell-peeled-off snails.
My eyes fill with tears;
smoke floats from my ears
and a few flames fly out of my nose.
My hair stands on end
and I'm tellin' ya, friend,
there's a right special curl to my toes!
I sip and I slurp it.
I belch and I burp it.
It slides up and down in my throat.
I've always recovered,
but no one's discovered
a formalized sure antidote!

Mr. Whimsy

STARTLING GLANCE
(in the mirror)

I have become a "turtleneck".
It's not the kind you wear.
Alas, it is a stretchy wreck
at which some people stare.
It leaves my chin and dives into
my collar bright and white,
but not quite fast enough I fear
to disappear from sight.
However, friend, it may not be
as bad as I've just said
because no matter what you see
it still holds up my head!

Who Put the "P" in Pneumonia?

BIRTHDAY GREETINGS

For years my brother's had a bent
regarding birthday measurement.
Since I turned "two" it *could* have been,
though he had not been born by then.
His theory's based on small black spots
like sugar cubes with added dots.
It works most years; not every one;
but when it does, it's kind of fun.
'Twas 6 and 5 two years ago,
which came with warning, "One to go."
He last year said, "It's *boxcars,* friend;
the measurement has reached an end."
I s'pose he's right. It's over now—
too many dots to fit somehow.
Today he called with thought concise
to bluntly say, "You're off the dice!"

Other Titles by
marc frederic (aka *Mr. Whimsy*)

Benny's Pets
Jenny's Pets
Denny's Pets
Timbo's Tale *of transition*
Beyond The Great Oak Doors
AbsurDitties/Trivia Chucklettes
Son of Trivia Chucklettes
Jasmine And The Snowman
Looking At Life Through My Left Ear

(out of print)
Rainbows, Butterflies and Other Assorted Edibles
Life Inside an Apostrophe
Strawberry Glue
The Enticing Wonder of Gaylan

Review the following website for book descriptions, information on marc frederic and World of Whimsy Productions, LLC
worldofwhimsy.com

contact marc frederic at
mrwhimsy@worldofwhimsy.com

INDEX

A BEVY OF HOT AIR BALLOONS (16)
A.B. SEAGULL (17)
ADVENTURE (56 & 57)
AFTER THE PARTY (63)
AMAZON AND THE MANATEE (14 & 15)
ANIMAL COLLECTIVE NAMES (26, 27, 28)
ANIMAL GOLF COURSE (10)
ASTONISHING (24)
AUTOGRAPH PARTY (45)
AVENUE OF THE REDWOODS (46 & 47)
BAD DREAM (65)
BAT IN OUR ROOM (58)
BAT WING STEW (167)
BIG PARTS (6)
BIRTHDAY GREETINGS (169)
BLOOD LEVEL (59)
BLOODY EYEBALL GHOULASH (64)
BLUE (25)
BRAIN SCAN (61)
BREAKFAST (60)
CAIRO (68)
CAT AND THE PRINTER (69)
CHANGING A HABIT (2)
CHASING RAINBOWS (70)
CHEEK SCAR (71)
CINQUAINS (66 & 67)
COLOR BLIND (55)
COLORED AIR (4 & 5)
COLORFUL FRIENDS (54)
COLORING (62)
CONTRAST (3)
DANCES (34)
DRAGON IN THE ARCTIC (35)
EASTER EGGS (37)
ELEVATOR ATTITUDE (36)

ENJOY (52)
EVIL WEEVIL AND THE LADYBUG (38 & 39)
EXERCISING (12)
EYE GLASSES (40)
EYES ARE FANTASTIC (41)
FEAR NOT (72)
FISH 'N MAN (73)
FIVE-SECOND LAG (74)
FIVE-YEAR-OLD LOVE (75)
FLOATER IN MY EYE (76)
FOLKS WOULD SAY (77)
FORCED-AIR HEATING (78)
FRECKLE COLLECTOR (79)
FURD (164)
GARDENING (43)
GIFT (48 & 49)
GRANNY RIDES A HARLEY (85)
GROWING AND CHANGING (84)
GROWING VOCABULARY (86)
HAND (13)
HAPPINESS HECTOR (23)
HE BE JEEBEE (87)
HERMIT (50 & 51)
HOME HUNTING (8)
HOW I LOVE PLAYING GOLF (11)
I COULD SIT ALL EVENING (53)
I LOVE IT UNLIMITED (19)
I THINK I'M IN LOVE WITH YOU (81)
I THINK IN YOU I'VE FOUND ONE (9)
IF I COULD HAVE THREE WISHES (18)
IF WE COULD VIBRATE (163)
IF YOU'LL (42)
I'LL LOAN YOU MY WHISPER (83)
I'M DROGGY (31)
I'M SO SORE (30)
I'M STANDING IN THE CORNER (88)
IMAGICATION (89)
IMMEDIATE RESULT (44)

INDISCERNIBLE (29)
INFINITE PATIENCE (44)
INFINITY (7)
INTRIGUING YOU ARE (80)
INVISIBLE BOGEY MAN (90)
IT IS BECOMING COMMONPLACE (91)
ITS ALMOST TIME (94)
JANUARY SECOND (95)
JUST ONE BOOK (97)
KIND SISTERS (96)
LICENSE (98)
LIFE IF FULL OF MYSTERIES (99)
LIGHT SAVERS (100)
LOOK UP (101)
LOST HEAD (103)
LUNCH IN THE SHADE OF THE SLURP (106)
MANDRILL (107)
MARSHA (108)
MEDICAL TESTS (109)
MIND MEADOW (92)
MOON BEAMING (165)
MY DOZEN COUSINS (110)
MY GRANDMOTHER'S CHANDELIER (104 & 105)
NAMING THE PARROT (111)
NEW (112)
NOSE, CONVERSATION WITH (114 & 115)
NTH (113)
ODE TO A RHINOCEROUS (116)
OFF WATERLEMON CAY (117)
OH, MY DARLING (118)
OLD SKIN (120)
ouch! Ouch! OUCH! (119)
PATTY (121)
PEACES (22)
PENGUIN DIFFERS FROM THE PUFFIN (32)
PIRATE, M.T. FLAGON (122 & 123)
POUNDAGE ON THE PATIO (20)
RABBIT HOLE (93)

Mr. Whimsy

RAINBOW BEING (33)
RAINY DAY (126)
RECIPE (124)
RecTangles (125)
REFLEX (127)
REMEMBER WHEN LAWMEN WERE HEROES (128 & 129)
RESPONDING TO A COMPLIMENT (82)
RESTAURANT AQUARIUM (130)
ROOM IN MY HEART (132)
SCAR THROAT (134)
SCHWA (137)
SECRET LANGUAGE (136)
SEDONA (138)
SHORELINE (102)
SHOWERING SHARON (140)
SHY, ROMANTIC LAKE (133)
SILHOUETTE (139)
SIMPLY AMAZING (141)
SLEEPY GIANT (146)
SMALL WONDER (131)
SOUNDS ALIKE (142)
SPARE TIME (143)
STANDOFFISH FRIEND (21)
STARTLING GLANCE (168)
STEEPED DREAMS (135)
STRAWBERRY JELLO (145)
SUGGESTION (147)
SWAMPMOSS MOSE (144)
TANGLES, GRAM AND ZOID (148)
TASTE BUD TALK (149)
TECH WRECK (150)
THANKSGIVING DAY (151)
TICKLEBUG (152)
TODAY I FOUND YOU WAITING (154)
TREMOR (153)
TRISKAIDEKAPHOBIA (156)
TROPICAL TASTE TREAT (155)
TWO IMPOSTORS (157)

UNDERSTANDING UPMS (158)
UNPLANNED (160)
WARTHOG (159)
WHAT ONCE WAS WHITE (161)
WHAT'S THE GREEN IN OUR GARAGE (162)
WHO PUT THE "P" IN PNEUMONIA? (1)
ZAMBOANGA (166)

Made in the USA
Middletown, DE
20 February 2022